Pirates Pinnacles and Petticoats

The Shipwrecks of
Point Pinos & Monterey Bay

BY
JoAnn Semones

The Glencannon Press

El Cerrito
2015

Published by The Glencannon Press
Tel. 800-711-8985, Fax. 510-528-3194
www.glencannon.com

The photograph on the cover is courtesy of the author. The illustration used on the endpapers is courtesy of Mystic Seaport, #1967/75.

First Edition, first printing.

Library of Congress Cataloging-in-Publication Data

Semones, JoAnn, 1945-
    Pirates, pinnacles and petticoats : the shipwrecks of Point Pinos & Monterey Bay / by JoAnn Semones. -- First ed.
        pages. cm.
    Includes bibliographical references and index.
    ISBN 978-1-889901-63-3 (alkaline paper)
1. Shipwrecks--California--Monterey Bay Region--History. 2. Monterey Bay Region (Calif.)--History, Naval. 3. Monterey Bay Region (Calif.)--History, Naval. 4. Point Pinos Light (Pacific Grove, Calif.)--History. I. Title
    F868.M7S45 2015
    910.4'520916432--dc22
                        2014043848

Publisher's note: Every effort is made to obtain and reproduce the best quality photographs. Due to the age of the photos available, some are of a lesser quality. They have nevertheless been used.

DEDICATION

For Julie Barrow,
who is my mainstay

By the same author:

Shipwrecks, Scalawags and Scavangers: The Storied Waters of Pigeon Point

Hard Luck Coast: The Perilous Reefs of Point Montara

Sea of Troubles: The Lost Ships of Point Sur

ACKNOWLEDGEMENTS

Great praise is deserved by Jeanne McCombs, Special Services Coordinator for the Monterey Public Library and Dennis Copeland, Archivist for the Monterey Public Library; Paul Van de Carr, Collections Curator for the Pacific Grove Museum of Natural History; and James Smith and Donna Stewart, members of the Pacific Grove Heritage Society's Board of Directors. Thanks for your invaluable help with the historical details.

Much gratitude goes to Robert Schwemmer, Regional Maritime Heritage Coordinator of the National Marine Sanctuary Program, who is always eager for a challenge. Thanks for diving deep into obscure research files to discover what surprises lie at the bottom.

Heartfelt appreciation goes to Ben Kuckens, Roy Tullee, and Emily Wilson for generously sharing their family archives, images, and legacy. History is created by people. And so, the stories we tell about people and events of the past are also stories about ourselves. Thanks for adding important tales to our maritime lore.

I am indebted to Gene Barron, self proclaimed armchair sailor and researcher extraordinaire. Through his acquaintances with early maritime notables, Gene has amassed a unique archive equal to the best maritime museum or library. Much of it is rare and previously unpublished. Thanks for opening your amazing treasure trove.

Most especially, my eternal gratitude goes to Julie Barrow, my faithful shipmate whose unwavering support, encouragement, and insight allows me to continue my maritime pursuits. I could not have completed any of my books without you. Thanks for sailing with me through roadtrips and research, presentations and palaver, and for always staying the course.

~ J.A.S.

CONTENTS

ILLUSTRATIONS

PROLOGUE

Maritime authors face many challenges in their work. Most especially, how does one convey the meaning of a shipwreck, the value of a light station, or the role that local communities played in our maritime heritage? JoAnn has found the answer — the link can only be made through a personal connection.

She is one of those magical people who digs through musty basement storage rooms, spends hours with microfilm, and seeks out ancestors of noteworthy characters in order to find a broader picture. She takes these threads and weaves them into the cloth that is California's maritime legacy.

We are so fortunate that she is able to bring life back to ships, their captains and crews, the passengers, and the communities who were often affected by a ship's demise. Through her books, JoAnn gives us a gift. She gives us back a bit of our American heritage.

Dawn Hayes, Deputy Superintendent
Monterey Bay National Marine Sanctuary
National Oceanic & Atmospheric Administration

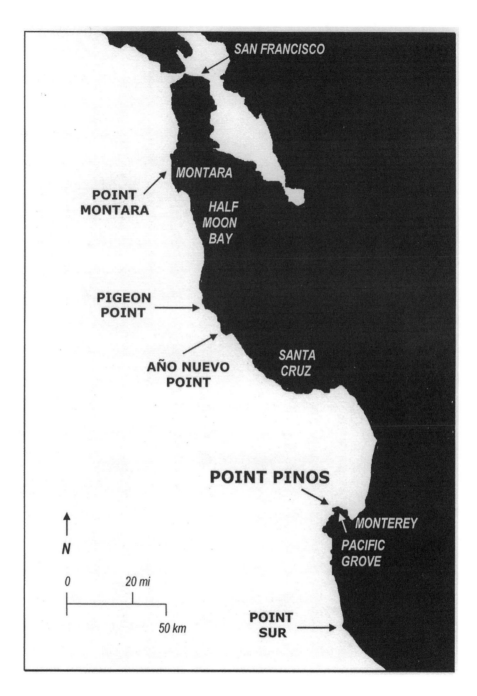

The central coast of California.
Courtesy of Janet Taggart.

INTRODUCTION

Referred to fondly as the "Circle of Enchantment," the spectacular coastline surrounding Monterey conjures up romance, poetry, and picturesque scenes. "Monterey is a little nest of quiet, encircled with an amphitheater of hills, pine-fringed and carpeted with flowers," an early writer mused. "The blue waters of the bay roll placidly upon the silvery sands, and the surrounding scenery is beautiful in the extreme."

While seeking a stopover for Spanish galleons returning from Manila to Acapulco in 1602, explorer Sebastian Viscaino encountered the bay he named "Monte Rey" in honor of the viceroy of New Spain, later Mexico. At the northernmost part of the Monterey peninsula, he also observed a thickly wooded area where native pines thrived near the water's edge. This he called Punta de los Pinos, meaning "Point of the Pines."

Later known as Point Pinos, the area was part of a large rancho of 2,667 acres granted by the Mexican government to Jose Maria Armenta in 1833. The property was re-granted in 1844 to Jose Abrego who sold it in 1850. By then, the United States had annexed Alta California, the territory was given statehood, and gold was discovered. Touched with "gold fever," fortune hunters and ships alike flooded into California, igniting cries for increased aids to navigation.

Jutting out into a sea where opposing currents collide, Point Pinos proved a dangerous and, therefore, ideal location for a lighthouse. Since February 1, 1855, its beacon has flashed nightly as a guide and warning to ships navigating the rocky Monterey peninsula.

Today, Point Pinos is the oldest active lighthouse on the Pacific. It is also a site brimming with a rich history of colorful characters, including Spanish adventurers, notorious smugglers, intriguing authors, gritty sea captains, and the first women lighthouse keepers of the West Coast.

Many types of vessels bearing many kinds of cargo plied the waters of Monterey. They included clipper ships, barks, whalers, steamships, schooners, and military ships. They carried household goods, clothing, furniture, barrels, dishes, fabrics, farm equipment, lumber, coal, tools, oil, dynamite, bread, fish, grain, sugar, wool, pelts and all manner of provisions and passengers. Some sought fortunes, others chased rum runners.

Shipwrecks come in many forms. They include groundings as well as total wrecks. They may happen when a vessel is under its own power or being towed by another ship. They are caused by fog, rain, sleet, heavy seas, unpredictable currents, rocks, reefs, fires, leaks, explosions, collisions with other vessels, and simple human error.

Shipwrecks occur randomly and are seemingly unconnected. Yet, there is one common thread. The ships were all part of a vast network of commerce and trade which spurred the growth of cities, supported the expansion of maritime industries, and opened new gateways to the West. And so, these isolated incidents connect us to a larger world.

Shipwrecks also humanize history. Often, there is something about a ship, a person, or an era that speaks to us or captures our imagination. Studying them gives us pause to study ourselves. Shipwrecks illuminate moments in time, they reflect the lives of those who came before us, they shed light on who we were and who we've become. Viewed this way, shipwrecks provide nothing less than a glimpse into our maritime roots, and perhaps, even into our souls.

1

GRIT, GALES, AND GRIEF

December 21, 1834
November 19, 1837
July 27, 1845
December 1, 1849

In the early 1800s, Monterey was filled with a vast array of ships bearing immigrants from Mexico, whalers from New Bedford, coastal smugglers, and Yankee traders. Four ships typical of the era came to grief in the surrounding waters. Their misfortunes led to the creation of one of the first lighthouses along California's coast.

Colonizing Monterey

In the 1830s, California was a thinly settled territory under Mexican rule. The region's chain of twenty-one missions had become its primary producer of agricultural goods. As Mexico gradually opened the coast to trade, word of the missions' growing herds of cattle drew ships eager to obtain hides and tallow in exchange for commodities such as sugar, chocolate, tea, and cloth.

Customarily, mission priests traded directly with ship captains. This practice began eroding in 1833 when the Mexican Congress passed a new law ordering the secularization, or disestablishment, of California's missions. The law also provided for the colonization of both Alta (upper) and Baja (lower) California, to be paid for through the sale of mission property to private interests.

1

Aspiring to "develop California agriculture and manufacturing and promote the export of its products to world markets," three wealthy Mexican businessmen formed an enterprise that became the first major attempt to colonize Alta California in over fifty years. The last effort occurred in 1781 when a Spanish civilian pueblo was established in what is now Los Angeles.

Jose Maria Hijar, Jose Maria Padres, and Juan Bandini created the *Compania Cosmopolitana* (Cosmopolitan Company) in 1834 with the idea of establishing a colony of immigrants on the California frontier. They set their sights on Monterey which offered newly available mission lands. The settlers would produce local goods for export while the trio would make huge profits, and hopefully, monopolize the growing California trade.

"Up to that time, the role of Alta California had been perceived as that of a penal colony or a land of exile," one writer commented. "Now the plan was to create colonies consisting of teachers, farmers, artisans, and craftsmen."

Shifting Seas

The company purchased the brig *Natalia* in Acapulco on June 21st for $14,000, payable in ninety tons of California tallow. Tallow was formed by rendering beef fat and molding it around sticks or pouring it into goatskin wine bags called botas. Known as "California bank notes," tallow was often traded for ships and cargo items.

Using his political influence, Hijar persuaded the Mexican federal government to pay each colonist a per diem and provide each family with a plot of land, as well as "four cows, two yoke of oxen or two bulls, two tame horses, four colts, four fillies, four head of sheep, and two plows ready for use."

The 185-ton *Natalia* set sail from San Blas, Mexico for Monterey on August 1, 1834 under the command of Capt. Juan Gomez. Participating in the expedition were more than a hundred men, fifty-five women, and seventy-nine children. Educators, agricultural workers, and garment workers dominated the group. Of the women, twelve were seamstresses, nine were teachers, and others were listed as wives, daughters, mothers, or midwives. Twenty-two year old Guadalupe Diaz increased the new immigrant population when she gave birth during the voyage.

The journey was otherwise uneventful and the *Natalia* arrived safely at her destination. As the vessel lay snug in Monterey harbor on the afternoon of December 21st, an unexpected storm struck, parting the ship's anchor chains. A customs boat raced to the rescue but capsized in the surf. Although the *Natalia*'s crew tried valiantly to control the ship, the brig grounded broadside, splitting the hull in half. Three members of the crew drowned.

A guard was posted to recover anything that might wash ashore, but local residents looted most of what surfaced. Spanish merchant Jose Abrego, who was a passenger aboard the *Natalia*, salvaged the ship's hardwood timbers for constructing his home. Casa Abrego, which soon contained one of the first three pianos in California, is one of the oldest landmarks in Monterey.

Abrego became a prominent citizen and held a variety of local political offices. In appreciation of his services, the governor granted Abrego the 2,667-acre Rancho Punta de los Pinos in 1844. Later known as Point Pinos, or "point of the pines," the rancho included a thickly wooded area studded with native pines and a rocky, low-lying point jutting out into the sea.

Ill-Fated Expedition

Aside from losing the *Natalia*, the three men who formed Compania Cosmopolitana were plagued by further adversity. Upon arriving in Monterey, Jose Maria Hijar had expected to succeed Jose Figueroa as governor. Due to political misunderstandings, the Mexican government revoked Hijar's appointment and dropped plans to give land to the colonists. In 1835, Hijar was ordered back to Mexico and lived the rest of his days in virtual obscurity.

A former member of the Mexican Congress, Jose Maria Padres ardently opposed the secularization of California's missions. He became embroiled in a bitter controversy with Governor Figuroa and was sent back to Mexico with Hijar. Nothing is known of his later life.

Juan Bandini fled to San Diego. Author Richard Henry Dana met Bandini on a voyage from Monterey in January 1836. Dana wrote, "He had a slight and elegant figure, moved gracefully, danced and waltzed beautifully, spoke the best Castilian with a pleasant and refined voice and accent, and had throughout the bearing of a man of high birth and figure."

Once established in San Diego, Bandini served as a member of the assembly, sub-commissioner of revenues, and a substitute congressman. The twelve-room home he crafted became the city's social center. Un-

Juan Bandini was one of three men who organized a voyage to colonize Monterey in 1834. They sailed on the brig Natalia *which sank in the Harbor.* San Diego History Center.

Author Richard Henry Dana met Juan Bandini on a voyage from Monterey in 1836. Bandini was fleeing political controversies resulting from the Natalia*'s expedition.* Author's Collection.

fortunately, Bandini's grand lifestyle and generous hospitality brought financial setbacks. Eventually, he was forced to convert part of his home to a store. Later, the building became a hotel which still stands in Old Town San Diego.

Meanwhile, the colonists never began, much less completed, their task. Left to fend for themselves the immigrants who sailed on the *Natalia*'s ill-fated expedition went their separate ways.

Pacific Whalers

In addition to drawing wealthy merchants and eager settlers, Monterey also served as a convenient port for procuring supplies. Many vessels, including whaling ships, dropped in to replenish provisions after lengthy voyages at sea.

One of those vessels was the *Commodore Rogers*, a whaler sailing out of New Bedford, Massachusetts. Whale-oil from New Bedford ships lit much of the world from the 1830s until petroleum alternatives like kerosene and gas replaced it in the 1860s. The busy port boasted as many as 120 square-rigged ships hauling in thousands of barrels of sperm oil and whale oil each year.

Featuring a copper-fastened hull, the *Commodore Rogers* was built in 1817 at New York. She made nine whaling voyages, all out of New Bedford, for T&A Nye and other members of the Nye family. Thomas Nye, Jr. and his younger brother Asa Russell Nye were part of a prominent New England bloodline of merchants, sea captains, and owners of crafts involved in whaling and foreign trade.

Having been at sea four months, the *Commodore Rogers* arrived in Monterey on November 2, 1837 with 900 barrels of sperm oil. While Capt. Henry S. Howland was ashore on November 8th, a tremendous off-shore squall struck the ship, causing her to drag her anchors out into deep water. Responding to the crew's distress signals, the French frigate *Venus* escorted the crippled vessel back to Monterey.

At dawn on November 18th, the *Commodore Rogers* left port with a fine breeze blowing. Later that morning the wind shifted considerably, slowing the vessel's progress out of the bay. By early afternoon, she was struggling through heavy swells. Although there was a light wind which had "every appearance of dying away calm," she soon lost the ground she had gained.

Late that evening, the wind picked up, blowing in squalls from the northwest. By daylight of November 19th, the *Commodore Rogers* had

Whaling ships such as the Commodore Rogers *and this one, visited Monterey often. They carried thousands of barrels of sperm oil and whale oil each year.* New Bedford Whaling Museum.

Between the 1830s and 1860s, whaling villages were scattered along California's coast. Remnants of whale bones, trypots, and a cabin are preserved at Point Lobos, south of Point Pinos. Author's Collection.

lost one of her masts. Realizing he was in trouble, Capt. Howland deliberately grounded the vessel to save the valuable cargo. The ship rolled, slamming broadside onto the beach and sending her two remaining masts overboard.

After the *Commodore Rogers* struck, a group of soldiers were dispatched to guard the wreck. Faxon Dean Atherton went to assess the ship's condition. Finding the rudder broken he remarked, "As she jumped and pitched, her deck appeared to move in an undulating manner fore and aft as if in an earthquake."

Atherton owned land throughout California, including a ranch in Monterey, and had amassed a fortune with his shipping and import-export enterprises. Thomas O. Larkin, U.S. Consul for the Port of Monterey, was a friend and business associate. Larkin had enticed Atherton to California by urging, "There is education available for your children and a dignity of living on landed estates that is convenient and accessible."

On November 26th, the remains of the *Commodore Rogers* and her cargo were sold at public auction. The 900 barrels of sperm oil were sold for $9,000 to Capt. Emmett of another ship, the *Castle Toward*. Most of the other items were purchased by John Coffin Jones, Jr., a businessman and the first Consul to Hawaii. These included the ship's hull, which contained 100 barrels of provisions, for $66; stores of bread for $10; 600 barrels of shooks (barrel staves) and ten tons of hoops for $283. The ship's masts, spars, rigging, and rails brought a total of $15,000.

New Class of Smugglers

Tariffs from foreign shipping formed Monterey's chief source of governmental revenue. These funds had been collected since 1814 when the first Customs House was established. However, many of the vessels visiting Monterey Bay in the 1800s were "smugglers" which purposefully avoided paying custom duties.

Often, import duties could represent a hundred percent of the value of the cargo. As a result, smuggling became big business and was popularly regarded by mariners as a legitimate part of trading activities. One trader shrugged, "Since revenue officials required no oath as to the correctness of the declared value, merchants and mariners prepared fictitious invoices, vastly under-valuing their cargo. There was a kind of understanding that this was the general custom."

Some went so far as to arrange to unload their ships at night, out of sight of local officials. There was one report of a $20,000 cargo from Honolulu which was brought ashore in the dark. Just enough was left on board so that the captain could pay duty the next day on goods assessed at $1,000.

Others went even further with their plotting. In this respect, the five-masted schooner *Star of the West* spawned "a new class of smugglers." Fashioned in 1840 by Ayles & Company of Weymouth, England, the 134-ton vessel was attempting to reach Monterey on July 27, 1845. Under the command of Capt. William Atherton, the ship carried a $30,000 cargo of household wares that included dishes, fabrics, and furniture.

Apparently, John Parrott, the schooner's owner and the U.S. Consul to Mazatlan, had purchased the products in Liverpool, England. Having obtained agreement from authorities in Monterey to take duties on only a nominal valuation, he planned to introduce the goods duty-free at Mexican ports, thereby realizing a large profit. One critic sneered, "The goose that was to lay this golden egg failed by a visitation of providence."

South of Monterey, the *Star of the West* drifted into Carmel Bay, striking the rocks at Point Lobos. Thomas O. Larkin described how the ship looked the following day. "I found all her rigging whole and sail set, washing against the rocks which were very high. The whole deck was under water, the railing of the vessel and chains covered with calicos of every color," he wrote. "The wreckers continued several days at work, bringing up goods sixteen to twenty feet under the water. I believe the vessel sunk immediately. The spars and rigging came to pieces during the afternoon I was there. The sailors are entirely destitute of food and clothes."

When the *Star of the West* was wrecked, Parrott's scheme went quickly awry. With characteristic grit, Capt. John Rogers Cooper, a sea captain and Larkin's half-brother, was first on the scene with men and ox-drawn wagons. According to an observer, "The creaking and screeching of the carts could be heard for miles."

Although three men were killed in the rescue effort, he succeeded in salvaging nearly half the cargo. Most of the merchandise was wrapped in waterproof oilcloth. Despite Parrott's protests, Cooper had his own ideas. He rushed the packages through customs as damaged goods, duty free. "Capt. Cooper made the biggest haul of the lot," the *American Trust Review* noted. "His technical knowledge as a master mariner enabled him to salvage, with ease and skill, an immense quantity of silks.

The smuggler Star of the West *struck the rocks south of Point Pinos in 1845. U.S. Consul Thomas O. Larkin described the ship's tattered condition. Her watch bell was recovered years later.* Author's Collection.

He reaped a considerable fortune out of the wreck."

Not to be outdone, Parrott continued accumulating his own fortune as a banker and landowner. During the heyday of mercury mining activity in the 1870s, he also held interests in two giant quicksilver mines. Biographer S.J. Clarke asserted, "He was to play a conspicuous part in commercial and civic affairs, and his record during the following years was one of great activity in various lines, his efforts being crowned with merited success."

Yankee Traders

Early in the nineteenth century, trading ships from Boston began visiting Spanish towns and missions along the California coast. They came first to barter for otter and beaver pelts, and later, for tallow, hides, and materials used by the natives and settlers. One man wrote, "Yankee traders scraped up all the commodities in sight and touch at Monterey, San Francisco, Santa Barbara, Los Angeles, San Diego, and other coastal ports."

One of these trading ships was the bark *Rochelle*. William Heath Davis and his colleague Jose Antonio Aguirre, who were prominent traders and ship owners, chartered her for one of the many trips she made to and from San Francisco. "In a short time," Davis exclaimed, "she was filled with goods and freight for different points on the coast."

Capt. John Paty, known for his spotless sailing record, was engaged as her master. He began his life at sea at the age of fifteen. Early accounts showed that "he seemed to thrive on the rigorous life at sea and to have made the traditional maritime leap from the cradle to the shrouds with relative ease."

As the *Rochelle* passed Point Pinos on December 1, 1849, the wind shifted unexpectedly to the southeast. Beating hard against the gust, the bark struck a rocky point and sprang a leak. Somehow, Capt. Paty managed to pull her from the rocks and come to anchor.

A few days after the incident, Davis arrived on the scene with his bark *Hortensia*. "The cargo of the disabled vessel was transferred to the *Hortensia* and she performed the delivery of the goods at ports south of Monterey as far as San Diego," Davis recalled. "The *Rochelle* venture, after the serious and costly accident, finally proved profitable."

William Heath Davis was an early trader and ship owner. He chartered the bark Rochelle *to carry goods from San Francisco in 1849.* San Diego History Center.

Capt. John Paty was known for his spotless sailing record. He experienced his only mishap while commanding the Rochelle. California Historical Society.

Having experienced his first sailing mishap, Capt Paty was less pleased about the outcome. Davis acknowledged, "He looked very much depressed when he reached the deck of the *Hortensia*."

Happily, the captain continued in a long career as a respected mariner and shipmaster. In 1846, King Kamehameha III commissioned him as Hawaiian Consul and Naval Commandant. In this capacity, Commodore Paty commanded both trading ships and passenger vessels until his death in 1868. A biographer reflected, "His reputation for reliable, safe transportation between Hawaii and the West Coast was an enviable one. He set a standard for all captains who followed in his wake."

Building a Lighthouse

By 1850, California had become a state and the discovery of gold had multiplied both the number of people and the number of ships seeking their fortunes. Tens of thousands set off for California by water during the first years of the gold rush. One of them summed up the hysteria of Americans in those heady times when he wrote, "An excitement as vivid as it was violent, seized upon the whole nation, like an electric shock it spread."

This surge of activity, along with increased shipwrecks, intensified the need for aids to navigation. In 1851, Congress ordered the Secretary of the Treasury, Thomas Corwin, to conduct a full-scale investigation of the Lighthouse Establishment. Based on a subsequent report, the ineffective Lighthouse Establishment was abolished and replaced with the Lighthouse Board. The board wasted no time in installing the superior Fresnel lenses in U.S. lighthouses, issuing detailed instructions for lightkeepers, and developing a more accurate list of lighthouses for mariners.

"The Lighthouse Board has not sought so much to discover the defects and point them out, as to show the necessity for a better system," the report explained. "Commerce and navigation, in which every citizen of this nation is interested either directly or indirectly, claim it; the weather-beaten sailor asks it; and humanity deserves it."

Corwin also oversaw the building of seven lighthouses in 1852 along California's coast. One was to be located at Point Pinos. For this purpose, the government bought twenty-five acres of Rancho Punta de los Pinos, then owned by Thomas O. Larkin and his associates. An additional sixty-seven acres were purchased later.

"The location is unusual. The ideal lighthouse is on a rocky headland, out of the reach of foaming breakers that roar about its base and dash spray against the lantern in stormy weather," a survey of the Monterey Peninsula declared. "Instead of being built on a barren rock, Point Pinos is located on the edge of a forest of pines and cypress. The greater part of the year, the weather is paradise."

The bark *Oriole* was dispatched from San Francisco with men and materials in 1853 and contractors were offered a choice of three sites upon which to build the lighthouse. Naturally, they selected the one on the southern side of the entrance to Monterey harbor which required the shortest haul for stone and other building supplies.

Major Hartman Bache, a distinguished engineer and later the Twelfth Lighthouse District Inspector, criticized the location. "I regret to say the result of this cursory examination was entirely unfavorable. It answers neither the condition of a coast light or a harbor light as fully as it might," he cautioned. "The light is soon lost in approaching Monterey, due in great measure to the interposition of trees."

Regardless of Bache's opinion, construction began. However, difficulty with delivery of the beacon's $1,600 third order Fresnel lens from France delayed the tower's opening for two years. On the evening of February 1, 1855, a light was exhibited from the tower at Point Pinos for the first time.

"The lighthouse is a gray, granite dwelling, one story in height, surmounted by a tower and lantern," the Lighthouse Board announced. "The light is fifty feet above sea level and will illuminate four-fifths of the entire horizon."

The opening of the lighthouse tower at Point Pinos was delayed for two years. On February 1, 1855, a light was shown for the first time. Julie Barrow.

2

VOICE OF THE PACIFIC

September 27, 1863
September 24, 1878

For a time, exploits at sea proved less dramatic than those on land. Once the lighthouse at Point Pinos was established, a series of colorful keepers crossed its threshold. One was shot by a notorious outlaw. The next became the first woman lightkeeper on the West Coast. Yet another was immortalized through a chance meeting with a famous author.

In the Line of Duty

Leaving behind his home in Oxfordshire, England, twenty-three year-old Charles Layton made his way to America in 1837. After enlisting as a private in the U.S. Army, he served with the Third Artillery in Florida and in North Carolina. He married nineteen-year-old Charlotte Ann Wade, a native of Beaufort, North Carolina, in November 1843. The couple was delighted when their first child, Charles, arrived the following year.

Layton transferred briefly to Maryland and to New York before setting sail for Monterey on the USS *Lexington* in 1846. Aboard was William T. Sherman, a new junior First Lieutenant and later a Civil War

*First Lieutenant William T. Sherman sailed to Monterey in 1846.
Aboard the same ship was Charles Layton, the first lighthouse keeper
at Point Pinos.* Generals of the American Civil War.

hero, who described the "very rough weather" that delayed their passage around Cape Horn. A few months later, Charlotte followed on the supply ship *Erie*, probably traveling with other military spouses.

Layton was discharged from his duties as an Ordnance Sergeant in June 1850 but remained in Monterey. By 1855, his family had grown to include two more sons, William and Thomas, and a daughter, Caroline. When the lighthouse at Point Pinos opened in February, he was appointed its first keeper at a salary of $700 per year. This was soon increased to $1,000 when he cited "the need to retain quality keepers and the high cost of supplies."

In November, Layton joined a posse of six men headed by Sheriff John Keating. The band was eager to apprehend Anastacio Garcia, a notorious outlaw who had murdered two men. According to an early newspaper, "Layton was keeper of the lighthouse which had just been erected, and loving a fight, had gone with Sheriff Keating and his posse."

More likely, Layton was selected for his military experience or he volunteered out of civic duty. In any case, the posse surrounded Garcia on November 16th, twelve miles from Monterey. In the ensuing gunfight, Layton was wounded in the stomach and hand. Separated from the rest in the confusion, he walked six miles toward Monterey before being discovered and brought to town. Although Garcia escaped, he was later caught, jailed, and lynched in his cell.

Layton died from his wounds three days later. One account noted, "As a legally appointed and deputized member of the Sheriff's posse, he became the second sworn peace officer of the Monterey County Sheriff's Department to lay down his life in the line of duty."

First Woman Lighthouse Keeper

At thirty-one, Charlotte Layton was a widow needing a home and a dependable income on which to raise her children. Many were sympathetic to her situation. The local collector of customs, who also oversaw lighthouses, contacted the Lighthouse Board.

"Charlotte Layton and her four children have been left entirely destitute. I authorized her to continue at the post occupied by her late husband," he wrote. "I take much pleasure in recommending her. She is industrious and bears an unblemished reputation."

The citizens of Monterey signed a petition in support of the appointment. When she assumed the position on January 4, 1856, Charlotte

Layton became the first woman on the West Coast to serve as a principal lighthouse keeper.

Some time during the next four years, Charlotte met George Harris. A native of Nantucket, Maine, Harris arrived in Monterey in 1846 as the third mate aboard the whaling ship *Sarrah Perkins*. He tried a variety of occupations, including ranching, mining, and tending a tavern and saloon. The two married in 1860, and he was appointed the new keeper.

There's little doubt that Charlotte was replaced by her new husband due to social conventions rather than any lapse in her lighthouse duties. However, the following year, George was replaced by Frank Porter. According to one biographer, "His removal was most likely due to poor keeping of the light as the Lighthouse Board strived to reduce the effect of politics on appointments and removals. Perhaps he was still more a tavern keeper than a light keeper."

After departing Point Pinos lighthouse, the Harris' continued to reside in Monterey. They leased and ran the old Washington Hotel. Built in 1840, it was the first hotel in California. For a few years between 1875 and 1885, they lived in San Francisco, but eventually returned to Monterey.

George Harris passed away in 1890. "Harris was one of the most respected and well-known citizens of Monterey," a local newspaper reported. "He was a quiet and unassuming gentleman, and his affable and courteous manner won for him many friends everywhere."

Charlotte Layton Harris lived another six years, having led an understated yet remarkable life. Along with Charles Layton and George Harris, she is buried in Monterey. "She was a woman of many distinguished traits," the *Monterey Cypress* declared. "Thus, one by one, the old pioneers of California go to make room for a new generation."

Next in Line

Next in line was Andrew Wasson. An ambitious lad of fourteen, Wasson left his home in New York in 1855. He sailed to the East Indies then rounded Cape Horn for San Francisco. "Imagining great wealth," he tried his luck at mining and making investments. He was serving as Deputy Sheriff of Monterey when he received the appointment to Point Pinos in 1863. Wasson was the first of the keepers to be on duty when a shipwreck occurred.

On September 27, 1863, the schooner *Julius Pringle* foundered at Point Pinos. According to the *Daily Alta*, "The schooner went ashore at

After her husband was shot and killed, Charlotte Layton became keeper of Point Pinos. When she married George Harris, he became the keeper. All three are buried in Monterey. Julie Barrow.

The home port of the schooner Julius Pringle *was New London, Connecticut. She went ashore at Point Pinos in 1863.* Gleason's Pictorial Drawing Room Companion.

Monterey Bay and is a total wreck. One of her crew, name unknown, was drowned in the surf."

In her own way, the *Julius Pringle* was a significant vessel. The two-masted, 94-ton schooner was constructed in 1829 at Beaufort, North Carolina. Her home port was New London, Connecticut which sits on Long Island Sound. Incorporated in 1784 as one of the first five Connecticut cities, New London was the colony's first official port and a key commercial hub. In the 19th century, New London was the whaling and sealing industry's second-largest New England port.

For many years, the *Julius Pringle* was engaged in New London's coasting trade. Although most of the early trade was with Boston, it soon extended to Long Island, Rhode Island, New York, Virginia, and Maine. Small ships like the *Julius Pringle* carried everything from household goods, clothing, farm equipment, hides, and buckskins to powder, lead, and military supplies.

In early 1853, she came under the ownership of Capt. William C. Talbot who was hoping to further the interests of his firm, W.C. Talbot & Company. Talbot had partnered with Andrew J. Pope in San Francisco where they unloaded ships and imported and sold lumber. When they learned of the vast timber resources of Puget Sound, the two joined with Josiah P. Keller and Charles Foster to select a suitable site on which to build a lumber mill.

Talbot had returned to his home in East Machias, Maine, to purchase the *Julius Pringle*, and obtain workers, equipment, lumber, tools, and other supplies for the new mill. After a challenging voyage of 171 days, the sturdy little ship dropped anchor at Port Discovery Bay in Washington's Puget Sound.

With the schooner moored safely in the bay, Talbot set out to explore the area. He spotted a sand spit at the mouth of Port Gamble which he judged to be ideal. The spit had room enough for a mill and associated buildings, plentiful Douglas fir, and was backed up by a large, deep water bay that could shelter ships from prevailing winds.

Along with a crew of ten, Talbot constructed a bunkhouse, cookhouse, and a store. Cut lumber he brought from Maine was used for the buildings which were roofed with local shakes. The foundation lumber for the mill came from trees at the head of the bay. According to one observer, "There was a charming replica of a New England village built around the mill."

A year later, the mill was shipping lumber to ports in California and across the Pacific. Talbot continued using the *Julius Pringle* to carry

William C. Talbot, owner of the Julius Pringle, *kept the schooner busy carrying lumber throughout the Pacific Northwest.* Time, Tide, and Lumber.

equipment, lumber, and supplies for the company's burgeoning trade. Talbot's reputation grew, too. A colleague acknowledged, "His activities and achievements are to be regarded as of the first importance in the creation and development of the lumber industry of Puget Sound, which afforded the foundation for all its subsequent progress."

When Keller died in 1861, Pope and Talbot bought out Foster's interest, thereby forming the partnership of Pope & Talbot. Within a few years, the enterprise became the dominant lumber company on Puget Sound. By 1881, the timber barons owned 150,000 acres of timberland, four sawmills, and nineteen lumber ships, as well as land in Maine, San Francisco, Oregon, and Washington. Within ten years they formed six additional companies dealing in lumber, trading, and shipping.

Dozens of Pursuits

Keeper Wasson remained at Point Pinos until 1871 when he was elected Sheriff and Tax Collector for Monterey. Subsequently, he served as the Sergeant-at-Arms of the California State Senate and engaged in mining speculation in Mexico before moving to Washington. There, he served as a Representative in the State Legislature and Customs Collector for the Puget Sound District. It appears that he found his niche. An 1893 biography stated, "Without fear or favor Wasson has pursued a line of justice, and held the office above reproach or scandal."

Allen Luce followed Wasson as lightkeeper at Point Pinos. Luce's log shows he reported the wreck of the *Silver Cloud* on September 24, 1878. He wrote, "This morning at 4:30 A.M., the schooner *Silver Cloud*, commanded by Capt. W.H. Siner, stranded on the sand beach two miles eastward of Monterey."

According to the *Daily Alta*, the 32-ton schooner had finished unloading a cargo of lumber at Monterey and was moored with a rope attached to a buoy. Some time during the night, her lines parted and she drifted about for two or three hours before stranding. All hands were asleep and remained unaware of what was happening until she went ashore. Lying broadside on the beach, the *Silver Cloud* was deemed "a total loss." Valued at $2,500 and insured for $500, the ship's wrecked remains were sold for a hundred dollars.

One day toward the end of 1879, a thin young man dressed in Bohemian garb presented himself to Keeper Luce at the lighthouse. Recently arrived in Monterey, author Robert Louis Stevenson was recovering from poor health worsened by a sea voyage from Scotland. Against the

The schooner Silver Cloud *foundered near Point Pinos in 1878. This is one artist's interpretation of how she may have appeared at sea. Note the vessel above is square-rigged as a bark and not schooner-rigged (sails rigged fore and aft). It may be that the term "schooner" was used to denote a relatively small, fast vessel, rather than specifically describing the rigging.* Gene Barron.

advice of family and friends, Stevenson followed Fanny Van De Grift Osbourne, a married woman, to America. In Monterey, he awaited her final divorce decree.

On this particular afternoon, Stevenson was rambling through the woods when he stumbled upon the lighthouse. Keeper Luce welcomed the stranger with his usual hospitality. The author memorialized their encounter when he wrote, "Westward is Point Pinos, with the lighthouse in a wilderness of sand, where you will find the lightkeeper playing the piano, making (ship) models and bows and arrows, studying dawn and sunrise in amateur oil painting, and with a dozen other elegant pursuits and interests to surprise his brave, old-country rivals."

Stevenson stayed in Monterey for a short time, moving to San Francisco, again to be near his future wife. Yet, the haunting beauty and power of the region stayed with him. In one of his essays, Stevenson declared, "A great faint sound follows you up into the inland canyons. The roar of water dwells in the clean empty rooms of Monterey as in a shell upon the chimney. Go where you will, you have but to pause and listen to hear the voice of the Pacific."

Author Robert Louis Stevenson stumbled across Point Pinos lighthouse while taking a walk in 1879. Later, he wrote of Keeper Allen Luce's hospitality. Knox Series.

3

SEALS AND SEA WOLVES

September 20, 1891

For twenty-four years, the schooner *Ivanhoe* led a rough-and-tumble life along the burgeoning waterfronts of Oregon and California. After surviving the rigors of hauling lumber, hunting seals, and bumping ashore near Point Pinos, she sank on a routine run down a river.

Unique and Enlivening

Perhaps more than anything else, lumber has been the economic mainstay of the Oregon coast, as well as its cultural hallmark. Most of the new settlers along the Oregon coast felled their own trees and sawed their own lumber, although some wood was imported by ship from San Francisco. The 1849 California gold rush sent the lumber market into a boom, and sawmills sprang up all over western Oregon, reversing the trade route.

The first sawmill in the Coos Bay area was built in 1853 or 1854. A year or two later, two of the Coos Bay area's most noted entrepreneurs, H.H. Luse and Asa Meade Simpson, raced each other to get their mills up and running. While Luse won the race, Simpson went on to create a

Marshfield on Coos Bay, Oregon was a busy lumber and shipping center and home to the schooner Ivanhoe. *The vessel was built in 1869 by John and Charles Pershbaker who also established a successful sawmill in the area.* Coos Bay Historical & Maritime Museum.

commercial realm so extensive that he became known as the "Lumber King of the Pacific."

In 1867, German immigrant John Pershbaker established a steam sawmill on the Coos River estuary, in the new town of Marshfield. Located near the top of the crooked arm of Coos Bay, the town was named by trapper James C. Tolman in 1854, after his old home town in Massachusetts. "He might have easily made it up on the spot," one writer observed, "so apt was the name for a town perched on tide flats and salt marsh."

Pershbaker's mill gave added stimulus to the town's growth, along with the store he opened. Managed by his brother Charles, the store was designed to meet the needs of men arriving to work in the brothers' new shipyard. They turned out vessels that included the tug *Escort No. 1* and the schooners *Staghound*, *Louisa Morrison*, and *Ivanhoe*. Soon, other sawmills and shipyards appeared.

Seen from the waterfront, Marshfield exhibited quite an imposing appearance. One historian wrote, "The large mill, the bay steamboats lying at the long wharf, the sailing vessels loading there, the active business portion of the town, and the pleasant residences in the background shaded by lofty evergreens, make up a picture which is at once unique and enlivening."

While John advanced the duo's business endeavors, Charles was elected to the state senate. Sadly, he passed away of pleurisy in October 1870. "In all his official relations he sustained a character of the purest integrity and his private life was unimpeachable," one obituary read. "No one knew him but to respect and esteem him."

Thrilling Experiences

John and Charles Pershbaker laid the keel of the two-masted, 119-ton *Ivanhoe* in 1869. Capt. James B. Magee assisted in building the schooner, as well as fashioning other vessels in their shipyard. Born in Ireland in 1841, Magee emigrated to America with his family in 1854 to embark on a career at sea. In 1859, after sailing on vessels of all types, he decided to learn something about their construction and journeyed to New York to learn the art of shipbuilding.

Magee found his way to San Francisco in 1866, moving on to Coos Bay in 1867. A few years after Charles' death, John Pershbaker sold his business property to E.B. Dean & Company. Magee stayed on with the firm as master of several vessels, and later served in a similar capacity for the Simpson Lumber Company.

Capt. James Magee assisted in crafting the Ivanhoe. *For many years he was identified with an array of shipping interests along the Pacific Coast.* E.W. Wright.

For many years, the captain was identified with an array of shipping interests along the Pacific Coast. Magee maintained a long, successful career building and operating schooners and tugs on Coos Bay and serving as master of ships which he owned. The home he crafted on Coos Bay is one of the oldest in the area and still stands today. When he passed away in 1918, Capt. Magee was remembered as "a faithful, fearless navigator who kept a cool head during many thrilling experiences."

During the 1870s and 1880s, the *Ivanhoe* was a regular caller at Westport in Mendocino County, California. Westport was one of the busiest shipping points on the coast from 1877 to 1895. As one of the numerous small, "dog-hole" ports along the rough and rocky coastline, it was also one of the most dangerous. Many mishaps and shipwrecks occurred here.

On one occasion, the *Ivanhoe* experienced her own thrilling moment. In the Fall of 1885, the schooners *Sea Foam* and *Humboldt* hauled under the chutes at Westport to begin loading lumber. The *Sea Foam* had discharged her freight and the *Humboldt* had taken on a couple of carloads of lumber when the sea turned rough.

Several huge breakers roared in, capsizing the *Sea Foam*, and killing a member of her crew. The remaining crew managed to swim out from under the capsized vessel and climb on top. Small boats from ships at the outer moorings scooted in to pluck the soaked men from their precarious predicament. Shortly after, the *Humboldt* parted her lines. Seeing the ship's distress signal, the *Ivanhoe* braved the breakers to rescue the captain and crew. Unfortunately, both the *Sea Foam* and *Humboldt* were carried onto the rocks and splintered like matchsticks.

Soggy Schooner

The *Ivanhoe* suffered her own mishap in 1891 at Moss Landing, north of Point Pinos. Keeper Allen Luce recorded in his log, "The schooner *Ivanhoe* went ashore at 4:00 P.M. on September 20th. The schooner left her keel on the beach, badly strained and waterlogged."

Commanded by Capt. Lundvolt, the *Ivanhoe* had arrived in Moss Landing from Mendocino carrying a full load of lumber. Moss Landing was an important early shipping facility and pier for commercial water traffic. Established in 1866 by wealthy Texan and retired sea captain Charles Moss, the landing shipped tons of sugar beets, potatoes, lumber and other products. Around 1890, a railroad was built between

Moss Landing as it appears today. Publisher's collection.

The Ivanhoe, *center, photographed at one of the many dog-hole ports in the Pacific Northwest.* Gene Barron

Watsonville and Moss Landing, increasing the volume and variety of shipments.

With freight still aboard, the *Ivanhoe* broke loose from her moorings and knocked a hole in her hull. Fortunately, no lives or cargo were lost in the accident. The Pacific Coast Steamship Company's steamer *Bonita*, arrived to take the schooner in tow. The *Bonita*'s master, Capt. Leland, made several frustrating attempts to float the *Ivanhoe*, but the huge hawsers parted like strings. After putting into Monterey over night, he obtaineded additional heavy tow ropes, returned to the scene of the wreck, and continued his efforts. According to the *San Francisco Call*, "The *Ivanhoe* was heavily laden with lumber which made it difficult to float her."

Following further attempts, Capt. Leland succeeded in pulling the soggy schooner off into deep water and anchoring her in Monterey. Given the heavy, lopsided cargo and the fact the keel was missing, this was quite a feat. The following morning, the *Ivanhoe* was towed to San Francisco for repair by the tug *Rescue* with Capt. Clem Randall at the helm.

The *Ivanhoe*'s cargo of lumber was consigned to the Western Beet Sugar Company. German immigrant Claus Spreckels had established a beet sugar factory in 1888 at Watsonville, a few miles northeast of Moss Landing. He also owned a ranch of 1,200 acres at Watsonville, all of which were sublet to beet cultivators. When he organized the Spreckels Sugar Company and created a factory in nearby Salinas in 1898, he merged the two businesses and went on to create a vast sugar empire.

The Watsonville factory included a refinery equipped to refine imported raw sugars. This kept the enterprise in constant operation. A report issued in 1890 showed the year to be quite productive. The product of the factory was 2,128 tons of sugar, netting the company $102 per ton, and amounting to an annual profit of $40,000. One trade magazine asserted, "Spreckels' Western Beet Sugar Company was the first U.S. beet sugar factory that was consistently successful from its onset."

Scrappy Waterfront Figures

After hauling lumber for many years for a number of owners, the *Ivanhoe* was put into service as a "sealing" vessel. While it's unclear exactly when the ship changed hands, it is known that she worked for Capt. Andrew P. Lorentzen toward the end of her career.

Near the end of her career the Ivanhoe *was used for hunting seals. The vessel sailed into San Francisco loaded with hundreds of fur pelts like those shown here.* Arnold Liebes.

Lorentzen was general manager of the Pacific Trading Company headquartered in San Francisco. Since 1865, he had been a "shipping agent, owner, and outfitter of vessels." In 1885, he added the fur seal trade to his list of endeavors.

Fur seals were hunted in the waters of the North Pacific Ocean and the Bering Sea. Sealing practices had been controversial ever since the U.S. purchased Alaska and nearby islands from Russia in 1867. The islands included the Pribilofs which were a principal breeding ground for the pinnipeds. Although the killing of seals was prohibited on the islands and the adjacent waters, a clear definition of "adjacent waters" did not exist.

Sealing was legal, relatively easy, and immensely profitable. A single voyage with a load of seal furs could net $10,000, considerably more than an average worker's yearly income. Usually, the hunt was a matter of driving the animals to a killing ground during the summer season. Poachers sought to maximize their profits by pelagic sealing, or killing the seals at sea, along their migratory route between Alaska and San Diego. Between 1887 and 1890, negotiations were carried out between Russia, Great Britain, and the United States but the parties were unable to agree on a basis for regulating sealing in the open seas.

Sealing was tough, unpredictable, and hazardous. A fortune could be easily won or a life easily lost. It was a profession known for legendary characters who were willing to operate on the edge of the law and whose activities often seemed suspicious. Lorentzen appears to have been among them, setting up his business in the free-wheeling city of San Francisco, and hiring hard-driving men like Alex and Dan MacLean to command his ships.

The MacLeans left their home on Cape Breton, an island located a stone's throw northeast of Nova Scotia on Canada's eastern coast, in the late 1860s. The brothers were among the thousands who departed Cape Breton seeking jobs, opportunities, and adventure. Their careers followed similar paths, sailing in the Atlantic coastal trade, joining the New England fishing fleet, and later voyaging out of New York on deep-water ships. At the end of the 1870s, they journeyed around Cape Horn to the Pacific Coast. Sealing was a new, lucrative industry and the brothers became successful quickly.

For more than three decades, Dan and Alex MacLean were among the scrappiest and most sensational waterfront figures on the West Coast. Favoring a Stetson hat and handlebar moustache, Alex was particularly formidable. His exploits spurred author Jack London to pen one of his

Capt. Alex MacLean worked for Andrew P. Lorentzen, the Ivanhoe's *owner. Favoring a Stetson hat and handlebar moustache, MacLean was known as a scrappy waterfront figure.* Greater Victoria Public Library.

most famous novels, *The Sea Wolf.* "MacLean had an exciting record of adventure and upon his deeds I based my *Sea Wolf* character," London acknowledged. "Of course, much is imaginary development, but the basis is Alexander MacLean."

A Few Bumps

Ships preparing for sealing cruises were usually fitted out for an eight or nine month voyage in January or February of each year. The cost of such a venture was about $3,000 which included provisions and subsistence for a crew of twenty to twenty-five men. In estimating the cost of provisions, water, and other supplies, Lorentzen's firm allowed fifty cents per day for each member of the crew.

The *Ivanhoe* returned from one cruise on August 8, 1892, arriving at San Francisco with 1,304 seal skins. Over a thousand were taken in May alone. Following the expedition, the *Ivanhoe* was laid up at Rio Vista, sixty miles northeast of San Francisco. Rio Vista was one of the many small ports which formed a bustling trade and transportation route along the Sacramento River.

"By navigation of the Sacramento River, the city has trade relations with the entire tier of river counties. The new comer will find a climate genial, bracing, and semi-tropical," an 1890 booster statement proclaimed. "No other county has such varied resources that are more easily or profitably developed. The outlook for the city and its suburban country appears to be the brightest. Sacramento presents herself as one of the most desirable and inviting localities of the Pacific Coast."

In the early hours of January 5, 1893, the *Ivanhoe* started for San Francisco for the purpose of fitting out for another cruise after seal furs. Moving down the Sacramento River under sail, she was caught by a strong current that carried her out of the channel onto a sandbar just below Rio Vista. "The vessel struck with sufficient force to carry away both masts, and every man aboard was thrown to the deck," the *Sacramento Daily Union* declared. "She struck broadside and the strong tide began to keel her over."

Knowing they had little time to lose, the crew clambered into the schooner's life boats, leaving everything they owned on board. Inside ten minutes, the *Ivanhoe* was bottom up and jammed hard and fast on the sand. "The schooner *Ivanhoe* is a total wreck," the *San Francisco Morning Call* reported. "She capsized in the Sacramento River and was dismasted. As she was swept on by the heavy current, a few bumps against the river bank finished the work of destruction."

Author Jack London modeled the key character in his famous novel, The Sea Wolf, *after Capt. Alex Mac-Lean.* Jack London Foundation.

4

FISH TALES

November 6, 1892
August 8, 1896

Usually, fish stories are filled with boasting, bragging, and exaggerations of the truth. However, these tales of canneries, salmon fisheries, and a woman named Emily all have a unique connection to Point Pinos Lighthouse.

Salmon King

When the *Alexander Duncan* steamed into Oregon's Siuslaw River on July 6, 1877, local newspapers exclaimed, "She is entitled to all the glory attendant on being the first steamship to enter that harbor."

At the time, there was little wonder that she made such a big splash. The steamer was built by the popular Dickie Brothers of San Francisco for pioneer businessman Robert D. Hume. Born in Augusta, Maine in 1845, Hume was the youngest surviving boy in a family of twelve children. As a toddler, Hume was sent to live with local farmers. Sadly, his father could no longer provide for a growing family on the meager earnings of a salmon fisherman.

At eighteen, Hume migrated to San Francisco to join his older brothers, George and William, who were testing the idea of canning salmon in tins. According to one report, "The cannery was a crude affair, and

In San Francisco, Robert D. Hume tested the idea of canning salmon in tins. Later, he became known as the "Salmon King of Oregon." Gordon B. Dodds.

William Hume peddled the first cases of fish from door to door, carrying them about in a basket."

In 1866, the trio moved to northern Oregon, opening the first cannery on the Columbia River. They continued to be innovators, introducing new machinery, canning techniques, and marketing strategies to the industry. By the early 1870s, their ventures had become wildly successful. Robert Hume married Celia Bryant, began raising two youngsters, and was running several of his own enterprises. Unhappily, he lost his wife and both children before the end of 1875.

Grief-stricken, Hume sold his holdings and returned to San Francisco. He bought the 371-ton *Alexander Duncan*, and searching for a new purpose, traveled along the southern Oregon coast. While visiting Gold Beach, where the Rogue River meets the Pacific Ocean, he purchased a salmon fishery. In late 1876, "he took up his career once again in one of the most isolated and desolate sections of the Pacific Coast."

Over the next thirty-two years, Hume expanded the cannery, acquired ownership of tidelands along the river, and increased his business interests to include a store, hatchery, hotel, saloon, sawmill, and shipping fleet. Along the way, he became known as the "Salmon King of Oregon."

Plenty of Consignments

Hume lost little time in putting the *Alexander Duncan* to work servicing his new venture. Having discovered that central Oregon's Siuslaw River was one of the state's most fertile spawning grounds for Chinook and Coho salmon, he dispatched the little vessel to its large shallow bay. She kept up a busy pace, making repeated trips to the Siuslaw to load fresh salmon, carry the cargo to Hume's cannery, and deliver the final product to ports far and wide.

For a time, she was commanded by Capt. James Carroll. Born in Ireland in 1840, relatives brought him to America as a child. He arrived at San Francisco on the clipper *Swordfish* in 1862, having gained early marine experience sailing from ports in Chicago, New York, and China. Capt. Carroll received his first command in 1870 aboard the steamship *Montana* and became master of the *Alexander Duncan* in 1879.

In 1880, the Pacific Coast Steamship Company purchased the *Alexander Duncan*. The celebrated enterprise was first organized in 1867 under the name of Goodall, Nelson and Perkins. When the firm reorganized ten years later as the Pacific Coast Steamship Company, it was ser-

The steamer Alexander Duncan *kept a busy pace carrying salmon for R.D. Hume's canning company.* Gordon B. Dodds.

Although the Alexander Duncan *struck a rock at Point Pinos in 1892, she was able to sail on.* Gene Barron.

vicing twenty ports in California. Although the partners of the company sold their vessels and controlling interest to Henry Villard of the Oregon Railway and Navigation Company in 1881, they stayed on as general managers under the newly-formed Pacific Coast Steamship Company which remained a dominant force in coastal shipping for many years.

The steamer made countless runs up and down both the northern and southern coast of California, "receiving plenty of consignments from shippers." The *Los Angeles Herald* even dubbed the *Alexander Duncan* "one of the best freight steamers on the Coast." Unfortunately, her good reputation could not always help avoid mishaps.

Carrying a cargo of hogs on September 8, 1885, she went ashore at Mile Rock near the entrance to San Francisco harbor. Capt. A. Nicolson, who was on deck at the time, insisted that the fog was very dense and no lights could be seen.

Brush with Disaster

The Board of Inquiry thought otherwise. Finding that the skipper misjudged his position while shaping his course to enter the harbor, the board suspended his license for fifteen days. "Capt. Nicolson is an able and experienced coasting master," they noted, "but in this instance, he failed to exercise his customary vigilance and precaution against the dangers of entering the port of San Francisco in a dense fog by neglecting to use his charts."

Although the *Alexander Duncan* filled rapidly with water, calm weather and smooth seas kept her in one piece. Fortunately, no lives were lost and a large portion of the cargo was saved. However, there was a good deal of controversy over the steamer's future. Some officials said it was impossible to estimate how much it would coast to put the vessel in good working order again. Believing that it could cost as much as building a new ship, they thought that the best thing that could be done was "to saw her in two in the middle and throw both ends away."

Fortunately, reason prevailed. The *Alexander Duncan* was raised and repaired at an estimated cost of $4,000. She sailed without incident until May 26, 1891, when a bar of submerged railroad iron punched a hole in her hull while she was tied up at a wharf in San Francisco. Mended in dry-dock, she set out again.

The following year, the *Alexander Duncan* experienced another brush with disaster, this time at Point Pinos. On November 6, 1892, Keeper Allen Luce reported, "Wind light, southwest, foggy, very thick.

The steamer *Alexander Duncan* struck a rock and made a big hole in her port bow. Discharged cargo and patched up the hole."

Attempting to travel from San Francisco to Santa Cruz three weeks later, the *Alexander Duncan* encountered a massive storm. "Being unable to make headway against a southeaster, she had to turn back," the *San Francisco Morning Call* explained. "The seas swept over her deck completely."

Her rocky sailing days came to a close in 1902 when she was converted to a coal barge. The *Alexander Duncan* was broken up in 1916. She had faced her final challenge.

"Socialite Lightkeeper"

Unexpected changes came to Point Pinos on June 29, 1893 when Emily Fish arrived as Allen Luce's successor. He had served for nearly twenty-three years. She was to become one of the most celebrated lighthouse keepers in history.

Originally from Albion, Michigan, Emily Maitland was seventeen when she married Dr. Melancthon W. Fish in 1860. The couple traveled to China where he was inspector of the Imperial Customs. In 1862, they returned to a United States torn by Civil War. Dutifully, Dr. Fish joined the Union Army. As medical director of the Sixteenth Army Corps, he served at the battle of Vicksburg and participated in Gen. William T. Sherman's famous "March to the Sea." Emily accompanied them as part of the Sanitary League, the forerunner of the American Red Cross.

When the war ended, Dr. Fish was transferred to Benicia, California where he resigned his commission. In addition to conducting a private medical practice, he held positions at the University of California as professor of physiology and microscopy and at Cooper College in San Francisco as professor of medical science. Dr. Fish was highly regarded and well known for his "reputation of being one of the best educated and most eminent physicians of the Pacific Coast."

As the young wife of a prominent man, Emily happily played hostess to their ever widening circle of friends and professional acquaintances. This came to an end in 1891 when her husband died suddenly. Needing to make a new life for herself, Emily sought the counsel of her son-in-law, Lt. Cdr. Henry E. Nichols.

Nichols, a former naval officer, was serving as inspector of the Twelfth District of the Lighthouse Service. Using his influence, Nichols recommended Emily for the position Allen Luce was vacating at Point

Dr. Melancthon W. Fish was a prominent
physician and educator. After he died, his wife
Emily became keeper of Point Pinos lighthouse.
Stanford Medical History Center.

Emily Fish served at Point Pinos from 1893 to 1926. She became one of the most celebrated lighthouse keepers in history. Monterey Public Library.

Pinos Lighthouse. According to one biographer, "At fifty, Emily Fish was a tall, slender, attractive, fashionably dressed woman who was to make many changes at the lonely light station."

In addition to bringing her Chinese servant, Lew Kew or "Que," Emily brought new style and color to the ninety-two acres surrounding the lighthouse. Thoroughbred horses, Holstein cows, white leghorn chickens, and French poodles roamed the grounds. Around the station, she added a circular fence, set off with cypress hedges, green lawns, and blossoming flowers. Inside, she took pleasure in entertaining officers of visiting naval ships as well as artists and writers from Monterey. One admirer sighed, "The book-cluttered rooms of the old building took on a rare beauty as her furniture, paintings, and old silver glowed in the soft light of flickering candles."

Although Emily was soon known as the "socialite lightkeeper," she was fastidious in addressing her lighthouse duties. A proper watch schedule had to be maintained, the light tended, and the buildings painted or whitewashed. To accomplish these tasks, she was authorized to hire assistants. The station was inspected frequently and Emily was always commended for its excellent condition.

Most of the men she employed as laborers were unable to meet her high standards. "Emily must have been a strict taskmaster as the lighthouse logs show that she hired more than thirty men in her twenty-one years as keeper. Most of them were discharged due to incompetence," a biographer revealed. "An example of her meticulous housekeeping was that she kept a feather duster by the front door for children to clean their shoes when they came to visit."

Shipwreck Sighting

On August 8, 1896, Keeper Emily Fish noted her first shipwreck sighting. Calmly and simply, she recorded in her log, "Wind light, westerly. Cloudy. Fog at night, thick. The steamer *St. Paul* ran on the rocks about 11:30 at night. Passengers and crew safe. Ship is now on the rocks close to shore."

A passenger and cargo steamship, the *St. Paul* was built in 1875 by the distinguished William Cramp & Sons of Philadelphia, Pennsylvania. With backing from his parent's shad fishery, Cramp was only twenty-three when he launched a shipyard on the Delaware River in 1830. "There were over a dozen shipyards on the Delaware at the time,"

In thick fog, the St. Paul *struck the rocks at Point Pinos in 1896. Onlookers gathered to view the sinking ship.* Pacific Grove Museum of Natural History.

a colleague wrote, "but Cramp surpassed them all with speedy wooden clippers."

As the Civil War accelerated the transition from wood to iron vessels, Cramp's yard continued to lead Philadelphia's shipbuilding efforts. When William Cramp passed away in 1879, he headed the most respected and extensive iron ship building concern in the country. The company's leadership was passed to his son, Charles H. Cramp. By 1895, the shipyard covered thirty-two acres and employed 6,000 men as machinists, wood-workers, molders, and riveters.

Family ownership ended in 1915 when the firm was purchased by a larger company which ceased operations in 1927. The yard fell into disrepair until 1940 when the U.S. Navy provided funding to encourage its reactivation. During World War II, the shipyard employed more than 18,000 wartime workers laboring an average of fifty-three hours each week.

For many, work at Cramp's became a way of life. The company's management took great pride in rewarding their employees' efforts by providing weekly lunchtime dances, creating sports teams for both men and women, and "offering hot food in the way of soups, meats, stews, vegetables, sandwiches, ice cream, pies, and cakes."

The yard remained a major force in the shipbuilding industry until 1946 when it closed its doors for good. Today, the site is an industrial yard but Cramp & Sons is still remembered as "the shipyard that shifted the focus of shipbuilding in this country from New York to the Delaware Valley."

Miscalculation

When the *St. Paul* struck the rocks south of Point Pinos, First Officer Andrew Hall and Capt. J.C. Downing were on the bridge. The night was dark with a thick, heavy fog hanging low over the ocean, making it impossible to see far ahead. Suddenly, one of the lookouts noticed the foam of a breaker ahead and quickly gave the alarm. The bell sounded, but it was too late. The doomed vessel struck the rocks with such force that some of the passengers were thrown out of their berths.

For a few minutes, all was confusion. Clad only in their night clothes, frightened passengers rushed onto the deck and into the saloon. While the cool-headed captain and his officers quieted their fears as the ship's forward compartment filled rapidly with water.

William Cramp. The steamship St. Paul *was built in 1875 by William Cramp & Sons. The company led Philadelphia's shipbuilding efforts for forty years.* American Society of Naval Engineers.

Despite valiant efforts to release the *St. Paul* from her precarious position, she lay hard and fast on the rocks. The order to lower the boats was given and the fifty passengers, who had since dressed and secured their valuables, were soon safely stowed away in the boats. James J. Wilson, the ship's engineer recalled, "They had two lifeboats and the women and children were taken off. One boat went to Carmel and the other to Monterey."

Capt. Charles M. Goodall, the *St. Paul*'s owner and a partner in the Pacific Coast Steamship Company, hastened to the scene to assess the damage. Like the *Alexander Duncan*, the *St. Paul* was one of the company's many coastal vessels, making runs between San Francisco and San Pedro. At the time, the three-masted steamer was the largest vessel of its kind plying the waters along the California coast. On this trip, she was heavily laden, carrying a $15,000 cargo comprised of five thousand sacks of grain and wool and over a hundred head of calves.

The wreck site left little to the imagination. Goodall found the *St. Paul* resting upon two jagged boulders. Faced with little hope of saving the ship, he ordered that "the work of dismantling the vessel be pushed with all possible speed."

To accomplish this, he sent another of the company's steamers to assist. The *Gipsy* arrived none too soon. As seawater seeped into the lower deck where the terror-stricken calves were fastened, eleven of them broke loose, made their way into the coal bunker, and drowned. With the help of the ship's crew, others were hoisted overboard and allowed to swim to shore.

Meanwhile, Capt. Downing was brought before the inevitable Board of Inquiry. Finding the captain guilty of "negligence and lack of skill," the board revoked his license. "The weather was foggy and Capt. Downing drove his ship at full speed upon the rocks, fortunately without loss of life," they commented. "Currents are not un-frequent thereabouts but he does not seem to have given the matter proper attention. Over confident of his position, he kept on at full speed in a fog."

Valued at $100,000, the *St. Paul* sank from sight. Keeper Emily Fish recorded the event in her log of November 3, 1896. "The steamer *St. Paul* fell to pieces, breaking in the center, masts falling at 7:30 to 9:00 A.M.," she wrote. "The debris broken into splinters picked up on the beach by the high tides and heavy surf."

5

VAGABONDS OF THE SEA

September 18, 1904
September 27, 1905

West Coast schooners could be called the vagabonds of the sea. These agile little ships sailed unceasingly, roved from port to port, hauled everything from lumber to liquor, and served many masters. Two of them met their share of misfortune when they foundered just a year apart near Point Pinos.

Filled to the Gills

During the decades between the Civil War and World War I, settlement spread rapidly up and down the Pacific Coast. Hundreds of tiny hamlets sprouted up along the shores of California, Oregon, and Washington. Accordingly, demand spiked for construction materials and all manner of goods necessary to support the otherwise isolated merchants and residents. To meet these increased needs, most of the products were shipped aboard schooners.

Schooners had many features which made them popular as cargo ships. They were crafted with shallow drafts for crossing coastal bars, unobstructed holds for carrying bulk cargo, and uncluttered deck arrangements for ease of loading. They also required smaller crews, making them economical to maintain. Schooners were speedy, relatively easy to handle, and well known for their nimbleness maneuvering in the tight coves strewn along the Pacific's rugged coast. One expert asserted, "They could be depended upon to push their way up the coast against prevailing winds."

The first two-masted schooners were constructed on the West Coast in 1861 and numbers increased with every subsequent decade. The first three-master was built in 1875 with the first four-master appearing in 1886. Over time, steam power was added and larger schooners were built for longer voyages and heavier cargo. West Coast shipyards continued to build sail-rigged lumber schooners until 1905 and wooden steam schooners until 1923.

These small, hardy ships were literally "filled to the gills" with freight. They carried coffee and clothing, fish and flour, grain and guano, lumber and liquor, mahogany and molasses, pianos and people, rice and railroad iron, soap and sawmill equipment, and much more.

Two of these vessels were the *Northland* and the *Gipsy*. They are examples of the stalwart breed of ships that gave extraordinary service, making countless runs up and down the Pacific Coast. Schooner enthusiast Louis Hough wrote, "They remind us of the thrill, the bustle and excitement when the call, 'she's been sighted,' echoed across town."

Shipping on Short Notice

When the steam schooner *Northland* slid down the ways in 1904, she was hailed as "a new, up-to-date craft capable of carrying 750,000 feet of lumber." Having been launched from one of the most prolific shipyards of its time, the Bendixsen Shipbuilding Company of Fairhaven, California, she was assuredly a sturdy and well-designed vessel.

Located at Humboldt Bay, the state's second largest natural coastal bay, the shipyard was created by Hans Ditlev Bendixsen in 1869. A Danish immigrant, Bendixsen was one of the most notable figures in Pacific maritime history. At age twenty-one, he went to sea as a ship carpenter, arriving in San Francisco in 1863. After working in various shipyards, including that of the distinguished Matthew Turner, he organized his yard in Fairhaven. Bendixsen sold his shipbuilding plant in 1901 for a quarter of a million dollars, having constructed ninety-two vessels for the lumber trade.

The *Northland* was built for Edward J. Dodge of San Francisco for his lumber company. The three-masted vessel was 195 feet long, 39 feet wide, measured 845 tons, and was designed to carry both freight and passengers. Dodge was the senior member of Pollard & Dodge, shipping merchants and manufacturers and wholesale dealers of lumber. Established in 1883, their immense trade extended throughout the Pacific Northwest.

Born in New Hampshire in 1836, Dodge went to sea at seventeen. He arrived in California in 1861, eventually establishing a mercantile business in Humboldt County. In 1883, he formed a partnership with Thomas Pollard. An admirer wrote, "Dodge is recognized as an exceptionally correct businessman. His cautious handling of his company's affairs as president has gone far towards ensuring its eminent success."

Thomas Pollard had been associated with the Pacific Lumber Company, one of California's major logging and sawmill operations. After leaving to conduct business on his own, he became a partner in Pollard and Dodge. A colleague stated, "His record as to thorough business qualification and integrity has never been questioned in whatever position he was called upon to fill."

When Pollard and Dodge organized the Eel River Valley Lumber Company as part of their ventures, they could not have imagined the magnitude of its growth. Over the next decade, they carried on an extensive manufacturing business with products consisting of rough and dressed redwood lumber, shingles, shakes, posts, and ties. They also owned and operated six miles of railroad which was used to transport logs and lumber "which could be loaded on vessels to any desired destination."

The capacity of the mills was 50,000 feet of lumber and 75,000 shingles each day. Most of this was shipped without delay to points on the California coast as well as to foreign ports in Central and South America, Hawaii, England, Australia, and Japan. The company gained the reputation of "having excellent facilities for furnishing and shipping cargoes on short notice."

Waterlogged

Expectations were high for the *Northland*'s maiden voyage on September 18, 1904. In command was Capt. Samuel Bonifield, who was called "one of the best known steamship skippers in the coasting style and one of the lumber trade's pioneer masters."

A renowned shipbuilder, experienced captain, and high profile owner boded well for the schooner's first journey. Unluckily, while making her way from Portland, Oregon to San Pedro, California, the new schoo-

During the late 1800s, the Eel River Valley Lumber Company earned the reputation of furnishing and shipping lumber products on short notice. Eel Valley Advance.

ner went ashore at Point Pinos. Keeper Emily Fish noted in her log, "The schooner *Northland*, with lumber and passengers, ran on the rocks south of Point Pinos at 2:00 A.M. Night clear, sea calm, Point Pinos light clearly visible to all on board."

All passengers and crew remained safe, but the ship's bottom was shattered and she filled with water quickly. The following day, the tug *Dauntless* began towing the waterlogged schooner to San Francisco. "Swinging wildly from starboard to port and almost unmanageable, the disabled *Northland* was dragged from Monterey harbor," the *San Francisco Call* reported. "There are twenty-five feet of water slopping around in her hold, along with much of her lumber cargo."

With all that buoyancy, the steamer couldn't sink. However, she slipped down into the sea until her main deck was even with the waves. There she hung. "The deck load of lumber is chained to the hull and cannot float away," one account explained. "The *Northland* could drift on the surface of the ocean for years."

After struggling with the unwieldy schooner for fourteen miles, Capt. Shea of the *Dauntless* telegraphed for help. Capt. James arrived on the scene with the tug *Defiance*. Like a pair of workhorses straining side by side, the tugboats pulled the saturated schooner to port. The *Northland* was taken to dry dock and unloaded. Damage was estimated at $15,000.

It was some time before the *Northland* was repaired and could continue business on the coast. Her maiden voyage had proved a terrible disappointment. A local newspaper added further embarrassment by commenting, "To be a success, a steamer in this business must have regular sailing days and live up to her schedule."

Meanwhile, John K. Bulger and O.F. Bolles, U.S. Local Inspectors of Steam Vessels, heard testimony from Capt. Bonifield and First Mate Peter Hedvall. The two gave conflicting stories about the mishap. The captain insisted that Hedvall tampered with his logbook and that he was drunk when the vessel struck the rocks. Hedvall denied the accusations, claiming that he had properly reported the ship's position.

Ultimately, the inspectors suspended the license of Capt. Bonifield and the First Mate for six months. Their findings indicated that the skipper failed to give explicit orders and that Hedvall mistook the Point Pinos light for the one at Santa Cruz, consequently steering a course to the wrong side of the light.

On her maiden voyage in 1904, the schooner Northland *ran on the rocks at Point Pinos.* Gene Barron.

From Passengers to Poultry Feed

Despite her awkward beginning, the *Northland* sailed on successfully for many years. In 1917, she was sold to Fred D. Parr of San Francisco. Born in 1885 on a ranch near Visalia, California, Parr attended business school in San Francisco before finding employment as a bookkeeper with the E.J. Dodge Company.

Noticing that most steam schooners delivering lumber to San Francisco from the Pacific Northwest returned empty, Parr began a business based on the improved rates he could obtain for cargo shipped on the schooners' return trips. Parr partnered with Charles R. McCormick who had opened offices in San Francisco and begun selling lumber on a commission basis in 1903. Over the next decade, McCormick would expand into other concerns, creating one of the largest lumber and shipping businesses on the Pacific Coast.

Parr's new venture was backed by his former employer and mentor, E.J. Dodge. "Old Mr. Dodge was not in good health," Parr's nephew, John Parr Cox, recalled. "He saw this bright young man with a lot of potential, so he gave him a chance by putting his money into the firm."

In December of 1917, the *Northland* inaugurated Parr-McCormick's new Puget Sound to California service. The steamship line also built a number of wooden steam schooners, including the *J.B. Stetson*, all of which could accommodate 150 passengers. Carrying six people to a cabin, conditions could be cramped. However, rates were reasonable. Passage to Portland was ten dollars with baggage stowed on deck, and another ten dollars with baggage placed in the cabin. At one time the Parr-McCormick fleet had thirty-five ships under ownership or charter. According to Cox, "They were the biggest factor in the coastal trade, particularly northbound."

Parr sold the *Northland* in 1918 to the Albers Brothers Milling Company of San Francisco. The schooner was put into service hauling oats, wheat, flour, stock and poultry feed, and delivering assorted cereal and grain products throughout the Pacific Northwest.

The enterprise was established by Bernhard Albers, a young German immigrant, who worked for an Oregon wholesale grocer. Having saved $15,000 toward creating his own business, and convinced of the opportunities in Portland, he persuaded his four brothers to join him in the venture in 1895. When Bernhard died in 1908, his brothers Henry and William took over the company's leadership. Over the next ten years, they added mills at Seattle and Tacoma, Washington, at Oakland

and Los Angeles, California, and at Ogden, Utah. By 1918, annual sales amounted to five million dollars. In 1929, the Carnation Milk Products Company purchased the firm.

"The success of the enterprise has been due to the adoption of several principles to which the firm has strictly adhered," a biographer noted. "One of these has to do with the selection of locations where rail and water meet. This was the thought in mind when the first plant was built, and the idea uppermost in selecting their last location."

A Dynamite Ending

The *Northland* was purchased from the Albers Brothers by the Atlas Steamship Company in 1921. Atlas was one of several lines of steamships operated by Pim, Forwood & Company. Born in Liverpool, Arthur and William Forwood took over their father's merchant business in 1862 at a time when the cotton trade was being disrupted by the American Civil War. The brothers made a fortune "first from wartime speculation and blockade running, and then from exploiting telegraph and cotton futures."

They set up offices in New York, New Orleans, and Bombay, and ran a small fleet of ships that traded in the West Indies and Costa Rica. They also immersed themselves in banking, politics, and multiple other business endeavors. George F. Pim, a merchant and native of Dublin, Ireland, joined the two in 1871. Atlas Steamship Company was formed and "for years it enjoyed a monopoly of American trade to many Caribbean ports."

The company was not without its critics. In 1890, *Vanity Fair* cynically dubbed Arthur Forwood "The Young Napoleon." The magazine chided, "By sticking closely to his desk, and by never going to sea, he has acquired a reputation for solidity and business aptitude. He is more practical than polished in his manners."

Tempted by a million dollar offer, the firm sold its interest in the Atlas Steamship Line in 1901 to the Hamburg-American Line, but continued to act as the line's agent. Atlas was the last British steamship line plying between America and the West Indies.

The *Northland* was used to carry assorted cargo, including dynamite, to ports near and far. Her work came to an end on July 21, 1927 when she collided with the British steamer *Pacific Trader* and sank in San Francisco Bay. The mishap was due to an exceptionally heavy fog.

The thirty members of the *Northland*'s crew abandoned ship and were taken aboard the *Pacific Trader*. Fortunately, no one was injured, but the *Northland*'s coasting days were over. "The *Northland* was loaded with forty tons of dynamite and nearly two tons of fulminating caps," one report emphasized. "That there was not an explosion when the ships came together was considered miraculous."

Nomadic Life

The *Gipsy*'s name proved to be an apt description of her nomadic life. Dashing up and down the coastside, she made hundreds of visits to numerous ports and landings without ever sailing more than 125 miles from Monterey. Launched in 1868, the steam schooner was crafted by the popular Middlemas and Boole of San Francisco.

William A. Boole and George Middlemas were both natives of Nova Scotia. They had an illustrious friend in Donald McKay, who grew up across the river from Boole's childhood home and who married Boole's sister, Albenia. In the early 1840s, McKay opened his first shipyard near Boston, Massachusetts and began constructing packet ships for the Atlantic emigrant route. Over the years, he also designed and built some of the most successful clipper ships of all time.

Having furthered their shipbuilding skills in Boston, Middlemas and Boole were eager to try their luck in San Francisco. Arriving in 1853, they specialized in ship repair, opening a shipyard in nearby Oakland. The two remained business partners for thirty-three years, constructing small vessels such as side-wheel ferries, fireboats, tugs, and schooners.

Middlemas and Boole fashioned the 293 ton *Gipsy* for Goodall and Nelson. Established in 1860 by Charles Goodall, his brother Edwin, and Christopher Nelson, the firm had modest beginnings. Between 1868 and 1871, their holdings grew to include several small sailing vessels, a number of coastal landings and warehouses between San Francisco and Monterey, and a large and fine fleet of steamships.

When the growing concern added George Perkins in 1872, it became known as Goodall, Nelson & Perkins. In 1876, Perkins purchased Nelson's share of the partnership which was renamed the Pacific Coast Steamship Company. Furnishing service to more than twenty ports scattered along the California coast, the enterprise would remain a dominant force in coastal trade for forty years.

Goodall and Perkins continued as owners of the majority of the stock until 1882 when they sold their interest to railroad tycoon Henry

Donald McKay built some of the most successful clipper ships of all time. He was a close friend of William A. Boole and George Middlemas who built the schooner Gipsy. The Metropolitan Museum.

Villard of the Oregon Railway and Navigation Company. Despite the sale, they stayed on as general managers of the firm. Goodall passed away in 1899. His colleague Perkins retired in 1915 and died in 1923.

Perpetual Motion

Early in her career, the *Gipsy* acquired an affectionate nickname. To her crew, and the occasional intrepid passenger, she was known as "Old Perpetual Motion." It was an apt description of a vessel running day and night, picking up or unloading cargo, wherever a landing or beach would allow. As part of the *Gipsy*'s regular schedule, she made a trip every two days from San Francisco to Monterey, no matter what the weather.

Monterey was an important port on the Pacific Coast Steamship Company's "Narrow-Gauge Route." According to author and historian David H. Grover, "Like its counterparts, the narrow-gauge shipping route provided transportation to places where standard sized equipment could not go, specifically, to small, shallow and undeveloped ports along the coast."

For thirty-two years, the *Gipsy* churned continuously along the central California coast, conveying cargo of all sorts. On October 30, 1900, the eve of completing her 1,717th voyage, the steamer came close to ending her career. Fighting strong winds, the *Gipsy* was hit by a huge wave. Seconds later, another big roller swept everything from her deck.

"We were past Santa Cruz when a breaker struck us," First Mate Richardson recalled. "The sea stove in three planks and knocked out the end of the deck house. The railing was carried away and almost everything movable on the deck was washed overboard."

Ropes that lay coiled on the deck were pitched into the sea and caught in the propeller. For what seemed a lifetime, the schooner was a helpless hulk drifting in a cross sea. "It looked as if the old *Gipsy* was gone," Richardson exclaimed. "The ropes carried overboard by the water went into the propeller and we were helpless. Luckily, the tug *Reliance* came along in answer to our distress signals and towed us into port."

The bulk of the *Gipsy*'s cargo was lime which can ignite when it becomes wet. Some of the casks smoldered and for a time it looked as though "Old Perpetual Motion" would go up in smoke. Credited with quick thinking, Capt. Leland hoisted the barrels overboard. Much of the rest of the cargo was secured by boats from the shore.

The Gipsy *traveled so often that she gained the affectionate nickname of "Old Perpetual Motion."* Mark Myers.

Broken and Twisted

Five years later, the *Gipsy*'s fate was sealed. Shortly before eight o'clock on the evening of September 27, 1905, she smacked onto a reef near Point Pinos. The schooner was on her regular weekly trip from San Francisco and was heavily laden with grain and other freight. Her master was Capt. Thomas Boyd. The *Gipsy*'s former first mate, he had been only one week in command.

The ship was overdue when she was sighted by the official in charge of Monterey's docking facility, a Mr. Norman. "When the *Gipsy* was within a quarter mile of the wharf, she appeared to turn and go backward," he observed. "She drifted outward and shoreward, finally landing on the ledge of rocks immediately in front of McAbee's Beach at a point halfway between Point Pinos and Monterey."

While Capt. Boyd sounded the ship's whistle, the crew tied two red lanterns to the mast as a distress signal. Within minutes, the *Gipsy* listed heavily to starboard. Fearing that she would flip over, the skipper ordered his crew to the life boats. Five minutes later, the engine room was flooded. In twenty minutes, the beach was strewn with broken timbers and sacks of grain. Somehow, Capt. Boyd managed to remain aboard for an hour before making his way to shore.

On September 28th, all that remained of the steamer was a few broken and twisted timbers imbedded in the sand. Her decks had burst open, allowing the cargo to drift away. Soon, the beach was strewn with assorted wreckage and merchandise. Keeper Emily Fish of Point Pinos reported, "*Gipsy* broke up at 6:30 P.M., much remaining on the rocks. The upper works came broadside on the beach and broke up."

The *Gipsy* had been carrying about fifty tons of cargo consigned to local merchants, including five hundred cases of beer. At a public auction the following day, the *Gipsy*'s broken hull was purchased for $25 by A.M. Allen of Point Lobos. J.B. McAbee bought the freight and wreckage that floated onto his beach for $11. It was a paltry return on a loss estimated at over $22,000.

Later, the *Gipsy*'s anchor was placed on display on the lighthouse grounds. It is the schooner's only remaining artifact, but there is no information about when or how the anchor arrived.

Ignoble End

The confused Capt. Boyd could give no clear explanation as to the

The Gipsy *smacked onto a reef at Point Pinos in 1905. Her captain had been only one week in command.* Pacific Grove Museum of Natural History.

The Gipsy's anchor was placed on display on the lighthouse grounds. There is no information about when or how it arrived. Author's Collection.

cause of the disaster. He noted that there was a heavy sea running and that the night was dark and cloudy. He also claimed that when he saw a red light, he thought it was the one to guide him into port.

The captain's report was reviewed by U.S. Local Inspectors of Steam Vessels John K. Bulger and O.F. Bolles. Both men were highly respected as capable engineers and conscientious officials. Bulger's later appointment to the position of Supervising Inspector would be "heartily endorsed by the shipping men of the Coast."

In rendering their decision to suspend Capt. Boyd's license for a year, the inspectors said: "There were a number of red lights about the town of Monterey that night. Some of them were railroad switch lights, and others were on city sewers being put in on streets near the shore where the vessel struck. The latter had only been placed there a few days before the occurrence. Capt. Boyd says he mistook one of these lights for the dock light."

"We are satisfied that Capt. Boyd was negligent and unskillful," they added. "When he changed his course, he did not give careful attention to the speed of his vessel or the time which had elapsed after passing the bell buoy. In seeing so many red lights, he did not proceed with caution, especially as he had never previously undertaken to navigate a vessel into Monterey harbor."

Other public officials were as unsympathetic as the inspectors. A local newspaper editor commented dryly, "This is a dangerous coast for navigators who prefer to sail their vessels overland."

The *Gipsy* was the oldest ship in use by the Pacific Coast Steamship Company and she had served them well. "In a sense she deserved a better fate," author David H. Grover complained. "Rather than experiencing such an ignoble end, she might have gone out in glory, battling a Pacific gale along the Big Sur coast."

U.S. Inspector John K. Bulger suspended the license of the Gipsy*'s captain.* American Marine Review.

6

SCRAMBLING SCHOONER

August 28, 1906

Another schooner mishap followed in the wake of the *Northland* and the *Gipsy*. She worked for an intriguing cast of characters and operated under one of the most well-known lumber and shipping companies ever established along the California coast.

"Horse Traders"

The Beadle Brothers were among the earliest pioneers of Pacific coastal shipping. It all began with Donald Beadle who arrived in San Francisco as "a buyer of hides." In the mid-1860s, he formed a partnership with Charles Moss, a wealthy Texan and retired sea captain. Known as Moss & Beadle, the duo built a wharf at Moss Landing, thirteen miles north of Monterey, to facilitate the shipping of hides, produce, grain, and lumber and to accommodate a small fleet of vessels.

By 1869, the wharf was buzzing with activity and the partners were managing a steamer and three schooners. One of the schooners, the *Jennie Thelin*, is said to have been the basis for the novel *The Sea Wolf* by Jack London. "She led a long and very colorful, though not always lawful, life as a hauler of varied cargos up and down the Pacific Coast," historian Gene Barron wrote. "She ran afoul of the law around the turn

A view of the offices of the Beadle Brothers. They were among the earliest pioneers of Pacific coastal shipping. Gene Barron.

of the century when engaging in an illegal seal hunting expedition."

Sometime prior to 1872, Moss left the partnership and later sold his interests to the Pacific Coast Steamship Company. Beadle continued on with new associates in varied shipping endeavors. He entered the lumber business in 1879, creating Beadle & Company. In 1888, he constructed a slide chute for loading lumber at Beadle's Landing, about a hundred miles north of San Francisco. The landing became known as "Nip and Tuck" for its challenging location.

Through 1901, Beadle also pursued interests as a second-hand ship chandler, ship broker, and shipping and commission merchant. When he passed away in 1907, Donald Beadle had seen his three sons follow in his sizeable footsteps. Although Alfred, George, and Donald, Jr., formed a number of lumber and shipping enterprises of their own, they were known far and wide as the Beadle Brothers.

"About 1914, the Beadles owned quite a number of vessels. With all those B's on the smokestacks, it looked like a regular beehive," Capt. Thorwald Oleson declared. "Their fleet fluctuated. They would have a lot, then, sell some off. They were kind of horse traders in the steam schooner business."

Captains and Cargos

The wooden steam schooner *Celia* was constructed in 1884 at Matthew Turner's shipyard in Benicia, California. Turner was a distinguished sea captain and shipbuilder. Born in Geneva, Ohio in 1825, he learned fishing and shipbuilding skills on the shores of Lake Erie. In 1850, he boarded a ship to California, seeking his fortune with hordes of other gold rush adventurers.

After two years of backbreaking labor in gold mines, Turner bought a schooner and began shipping lumber from the Mendocino coast to San Francisco. He expanded operations four years later, transporting cargo and fish from Alaska and organizing a trading company to Tahiti. To support his growing enterprise, Turner began designing his own ships. He completed his first vessel at Eureka in 1868, later setting up a yard at Hunter's Point outside San Francisco with his brother, Horatio.

The success of the yard led him to search for another location, this time across the bay at Benicia where he formed the Matthew Turner Shipyard in 1883. One of Turner's schooners, the *Equator*, was chartered by author Robert Louis Stevenson in 1889 for a voyage through

The partnership of Moss & Beadle built a wharf at Moss Landing, near Monterey, to ship hides, produce, grain, and lumber and to accommodate a small fleet of vessels. Monterey County Historical Society.

Matthew Turner was a distinguished sea captain and ship builder.
He constructed the wooden steam schooner Celia *in 1884.* San
Francisco Maritime National Historic Park.

the islands of Micronesia. The ensuing adventures inspired Stevenson's book, *The Wrecker*.

When Turner died in 1909, he had produced 228 wooden-hulled ships, 154 of them at his yard in Benicia. According to one biographer, "He was a hands-on captain, and a very capable one. He was also a very astute businessman. While Matthew Turner could have gone down in California history on the merits of his seafaring abilities alone, his greatest contribution was to the shipbuilding industry."

The *Celia* was destined to lead an itinerant life. Handed from one owner to another, she scrambled from port to port laden with all manner of cargo and commodities. Fashioned for George H. Collins of San Francisco, the schooner was 118 feet long, 29 feet wide, and measured 173 tons. Initially, she was used was as a produce vessel, carrying vegetables to San Francisco from south coast ports.

She was purchased in 1901 by the Beadle Brothers who employed her to transport lumber, railroad ties, shakes, grain, and farm products to dozens of towns along the California and Oregon coasts.

A Bumpy History

Hustling from port to port, the *Celia* was bound to experience a few mishaps. It's no secret that the sailing life of a busy coastal schooner was often a bumpy one. Shortly after her purchase, the steamer had completed loading a thousand railroad ties before the crew discovered that she was also carrying twelve to fifteen tons of dynamite.

The dismayed Beadle Brothers immediately discontinued the process until the explosives were removed. "It was feared that a sling-load of lumber or ties might drop onto the dynamite igniting an explosion," the *Mendocino Beacon* reported wryly. "The Beadles have no desire to have any blasting done on such a scale at the present."

The following year, the *Celia* nearly foundered while sailing from Fort Bragg, near Mendocino, to San Francisco. The schooner was fully laden with a cargo of lumber, cord wood, and telegraph poles. Heavy timbers were lashed to her deck. When a sudden southeaster hit the ship, the deckload shifted, opening the seams of her hull. Leaking profusely, she slogged into Point Arena for repairs.

Upon hearing that "the steamer was in a bad way," the Beadle Brothers dispatched their steamer *Brooklyn* to the rescue. Unfortunately, the weather remained uncooperative. With the *Celia* in tow, the *Brooklyn* fought through an increasingly severe storm. Rolling about in a rag-

During her sailing career, the Celia *scrambled from port to port carrying a variety of products, including vegetables, lumber, and dynamite. She is shown here on the building ways at the Mathew Turner ship yard.* Gene Barron.

On her final voyage, the Celia *was carrying 160,000 board feet of lumber. Nearly half the cargo was salvaged, but the schooner was a total loss. Above is a typical lumber loading operation of that era.* Charles Weidner.

ing sea, the *Celia* began leaking again. Near Point Reyes the tow line snapped, pitching her over on her beam ends. Believing that the vessel was going under, Capt. J. Hansen ordered all hands to abandon ship.

One life boat was lowered and cleared rapidly from the ship. The other was tossed into the water from the deck, forcing Capt. Hansen and eight of the crew to make a jump for it. As they leaped, a wave caught the skiff sideways, dumping the men into the roiling sea. Five of the floundering crew crawled back into the boat, while the others clung desperately to planks of wood and pieces of debris.

Although the *Brooklyn* sat a quarter of a mile away, the driving storm made it impossible to render immediate aid. The men in the waterlogged skiff used their remaining strength to pull for the steamer where all but three were pulled aboard. The courageous trio rowed back to those clinging to floating wreckage. After struggling for more than an hour, the rest of the *Celia*'s crew was brought to safety.

Hoping to salvage the ship, Second Mate John Samuelson and two seamen volunteered to carry a hawser back to the *Celia*. Once under tow, she headed for port. Hit by strong squalls yet again, the rope parted and was refastened twice before the journey was completed.

"Sweat and Hungry"

The *Celia* survived and was resold in 1904 to Swayne & Hoyt. Robert H. Swayne, John G. Hoyt and Frank L. Hoyt were colleagues in numerous business ventures, including the operation of a fleet of coastal schooners running between San Francisco and Coos Bay, Oregon.

Hoping to "join the rush to the timberlands," the trio also established the Swayne Lumber Company with a sawmill at Oroville, California. Located in California's Central Valley just north of Sacramento, the area was known as the "Land of Natural Wealth and Beauty." By 1917, the Swayne Lumber Company had become a major figure in the lumber trade. The firm's reputation grew when it established a right of way for a narrow-gauge railroad to carry logs from the nearby Merrimac forests to Oroville.

Since narrow-gauge railways were built with smaller curves and lighter rails, they were less expensive to build, equip, and operate than standard gauge or broad gauge railways. Narrow-gauge railways were particularly effective in mountainous or difficult terrain, making them popular in industries such as logging, mining, tunneling, quarrying, and conveying agricultural products.

Swayne & Hoyt was an anti-union company which pushed their men and their ships hard. As such, they became known as "Sweat and Hungry." Although local unions believed that "sea power is in seamen and ships are tools," Swayne & Hoyt had a different philosophy. Hustling crews and ships from port to port, they viewed both as mechanisms by which to turn a profit. Reportedly, the company's owners insisted, "Ships make money at sea, not at port."

In the years following World War I, Swayne & Hoyt were also engaged in the "tramp trade" with government owned ships leased from the U.S. Shipping Board. The tramp trade was one in which vessels did not have a fixed schedule or published ports of call. Tramp ships were contract carriers that could carry anything to anywhere, and freight rates were influenced by supply and demand.

Just months after Swayne & Hoyt purchased the *Celia*, she suffered a minor mishap. The schooner was hauling a cargo of redwood telegraph poles for the North Mountain Power Company from Mendocino to Humboldt Bay. After discharging the load successfully, she started back to sea. Leaving the channel, she lurched onto a sand spit. There she sat until the rising tide floated her out. She suffered no apparent damage, just a little embarrassment.

Criminal Carelessness

The *Celia*'s rambling days would end abruptly, four months after San Francisco's devastating earthquake and fire of April 18, 1906. Following the relentless shaking and twisting of the earthquake's tremors, author Jack London witnessed the developing firestorm. "I watched the vast conflagration from out on the bay. From every side, wind was pouring in upon the city," he wrote. "Thus did the fire build its own colossal chimney through the atmosphere."

As San Francisco and its industries initiated recovery efforts, the *Celia* continued her deliveries along its coastal waters. On August 28, 1906, the schooner was enroute from Santa Cruz to Monterey with 160,000 board feet of lumber when Capt. Newman lost his bearings in the fog. About two miles south of Point Pinos, he drove his ship bow first onto the rocks.

Immediately after the *Celia* struck, two boats were provisioned and launched. The first, with Capt. Newman and ten men, found her way into Monterey at an early hour. The second arrived several hours later with First Officer Anderson, the remaining crew, and several passengers.

In 1906, the Celia *wrecked about two miles south of Point Pinos. The captain lost his bearings in the fog and drove the ship bow first onto the rocks.* Pacific Grove Museum of Natural History.

The *Celia* broke up rapidly. The bottom of the ship was ground to pieces on the rocks, together with the lumber stowed below deck. "Another vessel has been added to the list of those that have left their bones on the coast in the vicinity of Monterey Bay," the *Monterey New Era* remarked. "It will take some pretty stiff explaining on the part of the captain to convince U.S. Inspectors that the cause of the wreck was not another case of criminal carelessness."

Although 60,000 to 70,000 board feet of lumber was salvaged, the loss of the ship and her cargo was estimated at $14,000. However, legend has it that more than just lumber was saved. According to the tale, the *Celia* was carrying some doors as deck cargo which broke loose and floated ashore. Earlier in the year, John B. McAbee had leased tent-cabins to a group of Chinese fishermen and their families after a fire destroyed their village. Residents salvaged the doors, nailing them into the front door frames of their tent cabins.

In addition to fishing squid, the villagers began collecting the waste products from the sardine canneries, turning them into fertilizer and chicken feed. Soon, the canneries took notice, launching a new source of revenue for the canners of Cannery Row.

The *Celia*'s salvage effort, both official and non-official, was not enough to satisfy local newspapers. "The coast in the vicinity of Monterey Bay has been the scene of several wrecks in the past few years, and it would be hard to find a valid excuse for any one of them," one editor commented. "Ordinary efficiency and vigilance ought surely to have prevented such wrecks."

7

OF CHIEFTAINS
AND CAPTAINS

April 25, 1909

A legendary ship with a mythical name came to a bitter end on the shores of Point Pinos. Christened for a fictional Scottish Chieftain created by Sir Walter Scott, her odysseys were as diverse as the captains who walked her decks.

Beautiful Iron Clipper

Her life at sea was as epic as her name. The *Rhoderick Dhu* entered the world as one of five magnificent iron sailing ships custom-built for the elite Waverly line of Williamson, Milligan & Company of Liverpool, England. Each ship was named for a character in Sir Walter Scott's "Waverly" series: Ivanhoe, Roderick Dhu, Lammermoor, Cedric the Saxon, and Kenilworth. Carrying lavish decorations of scenes and portraits from the novels, the vessels were widely considered among "the most beautiful iron clippers that ever left the ways."

The Waverly line's history was filled with prestige and distinction. John Williamson, a merchant and the company's primary owner, was later Chairman of the Standard Marine Insurance Company and a director of the famous Cunard Steamship Company.

Capt. Arthur H. Rostron apprenticed aboard Waverly Line vessels. Later, as master of the Carpathia, *he rescued survivors of the ill-fated* Titanic. Scribner's Magazine.

Many fine officers apprenticed aboard Waverly vessels, including Arthur Henry Rostron. Later, as captain of the *Carpathia,* he rescued survivors of the ill-fated *Titanic.*

Launched in December of 1873, the *Rhoderick Dhu* was 457 feet long, 40 feet wide, measured 1,534 tons, and was valued at $140,000. She was fashioned by the illustrious firm of Mounsey & Foster at Sunderland, England. The business had its beginnings in the 1860s when John Haswell established a shipbuilding yard to construct coastal brigs and schooners. Part of the yard was taken over in 1870 by the partnership of Iliff & Mounsey. When Iliff retired three years later, the firm became Mounsey & Foster.

The enterprise specialized in producing small iron sailing ships and steamships. They also made a limited number of vessels like the *Rhoderick Dhu* which became famed among the medium clippers of the period. Each was crafted to accommodate emigrants below decks as well as passengers in upper deck cabins. According to one sailing expert, "All had a good turn of speed and were powerful ships which would stand unlimited driving."

In the 1870s and 1880s, there was such a host of first class iron clipper ships making fast passages that it required a real racing skipper to showcase a specific vessel. A ship would spring into prominence for a few voyages, then at the change of skippers, drop almost out of sight. One historian observed, "Where so many ships were about equal in their sailing qualities, a particular ship needed to be either especially lucky in her winds or in her master if she was to be numbered among the record breakers."

Variable Winds

The *Rhoderick Dhu*'s performance received greater publicity in the 1890s than during the 1870s or 1880s. Her first few passages were to Melbourne, Australia with emigrants. Then, for some years she became a frequent visitor to India's Bay of Bengal, the largest bay in the world. Later, the California grain trade gave her the most employment.

Her first master was Capt. Robert Calvert who commanded her on her initial voyage to San Francisco in 1875. By 1882, she was also making cargo runs from Sydney, Australia to London, England carrying merchandise such as wool, tallow, leather, cotton, copra, meats, antimony ore, hides, and shale.

Launched in 1873, the Rhoderick Dhu *was a magnificent iron sailing ship named for a character in Sir Walter Scott's novels.* San Francisco Call.

For most of the 1880s, the *Rhoderick Dhu* was commanded by Capt. Robert Laurie Boldchild. Born into an English seafaring family, he spent his early sailing days with the famous "Loch Line" trading to Australia. Established in Glasgow in the late 1860s, the Loch Line was a fleet of iron clipper ships named after lochs or lakes in Scotland.

Unfortunately, the Loch Line's reputation was one of misfortune. Seventeen of the twenty-five vessels bearing the Loch name sank in accidents, disappeared, were wrecked or torpedoed in oceans and ports around the globe. As Chief Officer on the bark *Loch Earn*, Capt. Boldchild survived a disastrous collision with the French iron steamship *Ville du Havre* in 1873. While the eighty-five passengers and crew of the *Loch Earn* survived, the steamer was lost in twelve minutes, along with 226 passengers and crew.

Capt. Boldchild experienced a series of other adventures while at the helm of the *Rhoderick Dhu*. In September 1882, while on a voyage from London to Sydney, a severe gale swamped the ship, yet he skillfully brought her into port. "With some violence in the course of the storm, the topsail was blown away and damage done to the port bulwarks," the captain said simply. "It became necessary to work as well as possible against variable winds."

While on a journey through the Dutch East Indies in January 1884, Capt. Boldchild reported that the *Rhoderick Dhu* was "passing through large quantities of pumice." The strange navigational hazard was a result of the eruption of the Krakatoa volcano on August 26-27, 1883. The volcano collapsed in a chain of titanic explosions, destroying much of the island and killing over 36,000 people. For months after the eruption, volcanic dust hung in the air and chunks of volcanic rock littered the sea.

One of Capt. Boldchild's best passages was eighty-eight days from Liverpool, England to Calcutta, India in 1888. When he passed away at age sixty-three in 1909, he was hailed as "a fine old type of British shipmaster."

Swept Away

On December 8, 1891, the *Rhoderick Dhu* left Liverpool for San Francisco under a new skipper, Capt. P.S. Howe. Two other ships, the *Anaurus* and the *Otterpool* had departed for the same destination the day before. Naturally, this led to a great deal of betting in Liverpool on the result of the race between the three vessels. The *Rhoderick Dhu*

Commanded by Capt. P.S. Howe, the Rhoderick Dhu *encountered a storm off Cape Horn in 1891. The voyage was marred by the death of the ship's young second officer.* San Francisco Call.

proved her quality by beating the *Otterpool* by eleven days and the *Anaurus* by thirty-two days.

Three months later, she received a charter to load grain for Hull, England. Located along England's northeastern coast, Hull was an early haven of shipping and trading. Between Cape Horn and the Falkland Islands, the *Rhoderick Dhu* was delayed by huge masses of ice. For three days, Capt. Howe picked his way down a narrow water lane between immense bergs. At one time it was feared that the ship would be trapped among ice cliffs which ran sheer up to a thousand feet. However, the *Rhoderick Dh*u managed to keep clear and reached Hull in December 1892.

In 1893, the *Rhoderick Dhu* arrived at San Francisco on June 24th, having made the passage in 113 days from Dungeness, England. In 1895, she made her last passage around Cape Horn, leaving Liverpool at the end of the summer. Sadly, the voyage was marred by a fatal accident.

On October 30th, the ship encountered severe weather and seas off the Cape for several days. Her cargo shifted, causing her to list. Second Officer Gerald Scott Coney was on deck directing his watch when huge waves swept the vessel from stem to stern. "He lost his footing, was thrown down, plunged into the boiling ocean, and washed under the vessel," one of the crew recalled. "It was evident that he had been badly hurt and probably stunned, as he made no attempt to reach the lines and lifebelts thrown to him. One was thrown almost over his head, but the poor fellow did not see it."

As the crew began to launch a lifeboat, Officer Coney took hold of a lifebuoy which was floating near him. "Words of encouragement were shouted to him, but a heavy wave washed over the gallant young fellow and almost submerged the ship. When the waters subsided, he was nowhere to be seen," the *Liverpool Daily Post* reported. "He was a handsome and manly young fellow, and in every respect an ideal sailor. He had a brilliant future ahead of him."

The accident cast a gloom over the entire ship. Just twenty years old, Officer Coney had apprenticed on the *Rhoderick Dhu* and learned his seamanship skills from Capt. Howe. In the process, the two became close friends. According to one account, "The captain was very much grieved over the fatality."

"Well Kept Up"

The *Rhoderick Dhu* was purchased in 1896 by Capt. William E.

Capt. William E. Matson purchased the Rhoderick Dhu *in 1896. He dropped the "h" from the ship's name.* Hawaii History.

Matson who dropped the "h" from her first name.* Born in Sweden, Matson arrived in San Francisco in 1867. At age sixteen, he began sailing in San Francisco Bay and northern California rivers. Matson's life changed when he became acquainted with sugar tycoon J.D. Spreckels who asked him to serve as skipper on one of the family yachts.

Spreckels assisted Matson in obtaining his first ship in 1882. Matson sailed his three-masted schooner from San Francisco to Hilo, Hawaii, carrying three hundred tons of food, sugar, plantation supplies, and general merchandise. The voyage was the birth of the Matson Navigation Company and a long association with the islands.

Matson employed the *Roderick Dhu* in the Hawaiian sugar trade. For years, she kept up a steady, almost monotonous pace carrying freight to Hilo. Trade papers noted, "Although well on in years, she was still one of the handsomest ships on the Pacific Coast, and frequently carried passengers to the islands, being both well sailed and well kept up."

On January 29, 1898, under Capt. Charles Rock, she arrived at Hilo, just nine days from San Francisco, beating a recent record set by the *Henry B. Hyde* between San Francisco and Honolulu. It was quite a feat for the time, given that the *Henry B. Hyde* set several sailing records in the late 1890s. On one occasion, she made the trip from San Francisco to Liverpool in a brisk 102 days. On another, she set the record for the fastest trip from New York to San Francisco to England and back to New York.

Later that year, Capt. Rock retired from the sea and turned to farming. For nearly fifty years, he had been a seaman. For more than half of that, he sailed in and out of the Golden Gate as master of San Francisco owned vessels. "He now thinks he's entitled to a rest," the *San Francisco Call* commented. "Although he has taken to farming, Capt. Rock will not turn his back altogether on the sea. He still retains his interests in at least a dozen vessels."

Ocean Waifs

Capt. Rock was succeeded by Capt. Peter Johnson. Born in 1863, Johnson answered the call of the sea at age fourteen, shipping out as a cook on a Swedish sailing vessel. He joined the crew of the full-rigged

---

*   Although Scott's poem spells the first name without an "h," it was just as commonly spelled "Rhoderick" on pub signs, whisky bottles and as a first name among Scotsmen.

Peter Johnson served aboard the infamous T.F. Oakes *when this woman,*
Mrs. C.J. Hicks was born. Later he became captain of the Roderick Dhu. The
Oregonian.

American ship *Great Republic*, then the largest ship afloat, traveling with her to Boston, Massachusetts. For several years, Johnson sailed the seven seas, touching every large port in the world. He wrote, "I can't remember the day when I wasn't in or around ships."

Johnson also served on the infamous *T.F. Oakes* between San Francisco and Hull, England in 1884. One of only three large full-rigged iron ships ever built in the United States, the *T.F. Oakes* went on to become one of the most notorious ships to ever sail.

During the voyage, a baby was born. "Naturally, I can't remember anything about the trip, but my mother told me later that it was a rough one," Mrs. C.J. Hicks recalled. "The ship got into some jam or other and never made a trip after without some jinx."

Soon after, Johnson met William E. Matson and spent the rest of his career in Matson's employ. He set a breezy pace on the *Roderick Dhu*, making one trip from San Francisco to Hilo in nine-and-a-half days when other vessels were averaging twenty. Although Capt. Johnson soon gained a reputation as "one of the ablest of the present generation of ship masters," he credited his ship and crew for much of the success. "The *Roderick Dhu* was a wonderful ship," he declared. "She was a fast sailer and I had good officers, so we made good time."

During two of his voyages, the captain observed unusual instances of birds taking refuge on the *Roderick Dhu*. In May or June of 1897, a brown hawk boarded about two hundred miles outbound from Hilo and stayed for the duration of the trip to California. The bird made excursions to prey for food, but always returned to its same perch on the ship.

In October of 1900, some five hundred miles from the Hawaiian Islands, an owl alighted in the *Roderick Dhu*'s rigging. The bird was so fatigued that it was easily caught by hand and placed in a coop. Unhappily, the owl refused to eat and died within a week. No doubt the little waif was given a proper burial at sea.

An Omen

As Matson expanded his fleet, he introduced some dramatic maritime innovations to some of his vessels. The first Matson steamship, the *Enterprise*, was the first offshore ship in the Pacific to burn oil instead of coal. In 1900, the *Roderick Dhu* was the first ship to be fitted with electricity and a cold storage plant. "He could see farther than any man I ever met," Johnson said of Matson. "I admired him tremendously for it."

The *Roderick Dhu* continued along in the thriving Hawaii trade, hauling her usual cargo as well as hefty equipment to build new sugar mills. In 1905, she was acquired by the Associated Oil Company when it purchased Matson's Pacific Oil & Transportation Company. Matson's fleet of vessels and fuel oil tanks on San Francisco Bay formed the nucleus of Associated Oil's new marine transportation department. The total carrying capacity of this original fleet, which consisted of the *Roderick Dhu, Marion Chilcott, Rosecrans, Santiago, Monterey,* and *Falls of Clyde*, was about 80,000 barrels.

The *Roderick Dhu* faced a major transition when her owners converted her to a barge for carrying bulk oil. She settled down to a peaceful life, being towed by various tugs back and forth between San Francisco and Southern California. All was serene until the morning of January 21, 1909. Tied up at the Redondo Beach Wharf near Los Angeles, heavy seas proved too much for the *Roderick Dhu*'s mooring lines. In minutes, she was pitched ashore. Her skipper, Capt. W. Z. Haskins, attributed the episode to the "peril of the sea." The captain would later create active shipbuilding and lumber enterprises which served ports in the Pacific Northwest.

A wharf crew, under the direction of Superintendent M.T. Maddex, passed a line to the vessel, attached it to the switch engine of a locomotive, and attempted to pull her off the sand. The first attempt failed when the line parted. A second line was secured on the barge, this time attached to her stern. The *Roderick Dhu* was re-floated successfully "none the worse for her experience." The tug *Navigator* took over, towing the barge and her cargo on to San Francisco.

Her return trip was equally eventful. Heavily laden with oil, the *Roderick Dhu* was attempting to leave San Francisco on January 23rd when she was encountered a furious gale. A huge wave swept over the stern, parting the tow line, smashing the ship's wheel, and carrying two seamen overboard. The tug *Hercules* was sent to secure another hawser while the revenue cutter *McCulloch* took the ship's officers and crew aboard. The sailors, Charles Verdich and John Maher, were retrieved from the sea. Badly injured, they were taken to the harbor hospital for emergency treatment. The journey was an omen of more terrible things to come.

Mortally Wounded

For nearly three months, the *Roderick Dhu* continued transporting

The Roderick Dhu *wrecked south of Point Pinos in 1909. Pinned on the rocks, she disintegrated into a watery grave.* Pacific Grove Museum of Natural History.

oil on the California coast. In the early morning hours of April 25, 1909, the barge was being towed by the 204-ton tug *Relief.* The tug's master, Capt. Marshall, thought he was guiding the vessels toward the entrance to Monterey Bay when he mistakenly entered a rocky inlet. Realizing his error, the skipper swung the tug around and headed for open sea.

Unluckily, the towing cables snapped, and having no power of her own, the *Roderick Dhu* drove onto the rocks. As her iron hull ground to a halt, Capt. Haskins ordered the anchors dropped to prevent her from being carried further inshore. The skipper and his crew made their way safely off the wreck and quickly established a camp on the beach to prevent piracy.

From Point Pinos, Keeper Emily Fish reported, "Partly clear, drifting fog. The *Roderick Dhu* went ashore at high tide a mile and a quarter south of the lighthouse." Although Emily Fish would remain at Point Pinos for another five years, this would be her last shipwreck entry. When she passed away at the age of eighty-eight in 1931, she had not been forgotten. "She had a host of friends among those who visited the lighthouse, and often received visits from them after she had resigned from her station," the *Pacific Grove Tribune* commented. "In her experiences during her years of service were many adventures which she could relate in a graphic manner."

From San Francisco, Associated Oil Company dispatched the 155-ton tug *Defiance* to aid the *Relief* in a rescue attempt. Together, the two tugs attempted to haul the barge from the rocks during the incoming high tide. Unfortunately, the combined horsepower of the tugs only caused the *Roderick Dhu* to list toward the breakers. The helpless vessel sat broadside to the beach with rocks piercing her hull. Just like the embattled Chieftain for whom she was named, the *Roderick Dhu* lay mortally wounded.

In the ensuing days, Associated Oil made several dogged attempts to re-float the damaged vessel. The steamer *Greenwood* arrived with wrecking apparatus and the revenue cutter *McCulloch* brought life saving equipment. With the *Roderick Dhu* valued at $175,000, a final effort was made to keep her intact. Divers attempted repairs, but this too, proved unsuccessful. As a last resort, holes were cut in the side of the hull to extract cargo, machinery, and anything else of use.

Meanwhile, Capt. Norman Nelson of the Golden Gate Life-Saving Station arrived. Although Capt. Nelson had been station chief for only a year, he and his intrepid crew participated in many notable rescues and were lauded often for their courage and attention to duty. "We are paid

Capt. Norman Nelson and the crew of the Golden Gate Life-Saving Station aided stranded survivors of the Roderick Dhu. Overland Monthly.

by Uncle Sam to be life-savers," Capt. Nelson asserted. "That means we must save lives. I have taught the men that the first thing to consider, in all cases, is the saving of life."

Once satisfied that no lives were in danger, the captain and his men gathered food and cooking equipment from the wreck for the stranded survivors. When Capt. Nelson learned that the shipwrecked mariners had left their clothing and personal property aboard, he returned again. He also ran lines from the *Roderick Dhu* to the beach so those ashore could reach the vessel as necessary in perfect safety.

Credited with being "the hero of the wreck," Capt. Nelson appropriated a souvenir for the life saving station – the ship's figurehead. What remained of the *Roderick Dhu* was abandoned and gradually disintegrated under the pounding surf. According to one local writer, "Rocks and winds and seas collapsed the big steel hull of the *Roderick Dhu* who joined her predecessors in their watery graves."

Capt. Nelson and his life-saving crew also salvaged a fragment of the Roderick Dhu's *figurehead.* San Francisco Maritime National Historic Park.

8

WHISTLING IN THE DARK

December 14, 1923
May 3, 1924

Two vessels, as different as they could be, foundered at Point Pinos within five months of each other. Aside from being bound together by place and time, they shared ties to one man who served aboard both.

Knocking About

Born in northern Germany in 1898, Bernhard G. Kuckens typified the crewmen who served aboard multiple vessels. Like so many others, he lived a rather nomadic life, making his way as best he could. He knocked about on ships of all types, plying the bustling coastal waters along California, Oregon, and Washington. In most cases, he hired on for a few months at a time. According to his son Ben Kuckens, "It was a hard way of life, but he loved the sea."

Kuckens sought out the sea at an early age. At his father's death in 1912, he was sent to live with an uncle who was described as "a strict schoolmaster." The young Kuckens ran away, shipping out as a deckboy on the three-masted sailing ship *Rigel*. In 1914, he signed on as an able-bodied seaman with the *Hans*, a large iron hulled, four-masted bark.

After the outbreak of World War I, he made his way to San Francisco and onto the wooden steam schooner *Klamath*. Built by J.H. Price at

Bernhard G. Kuckens received his alien seaman's identification card in 1919. He served on many vessels, including the schooner Flavel *and the tanker* Frank H. Buck. Ben Kuckens.

Fairhaven, California in 1910, the 1,038-ton vessel was part of the noteworthy McCormick Lumber Company's fleet. According to one source, the fleet's owner, Charles R. McCormick, "bought a ship he didn't have money to pay for and began a business career that made him millions."

Kuckens served on vessels that included the tanker *Frank H. Buck* in 1919, as well as the lumber schooners *Flavel* in 1920 and *J.B. Stetson* in 1925. Each of these ships came to grief at Point Pinos: the *Flavel* in 1923, the *Frank H, Buck* in 1924, and the *J.B. Stetson* in 1934. Although Kuckens wasn't aboard at the time they wrecked, he suffered a narrow escape in the opening days of World War II.

He was second mate on the freighter *Lahaina* when it was shelled by a Japanese submarine on December 11, 1941. Under constant fire, the entire crew of thirty-four escaped into a single lifeboat. According to Third Assistant Engineer Michael P. Locke, "The ship was about nine hundred miles offshore at the time of the sinking. The lifeboat remained on site and returned to the ship to retrieve additional supplies but had to leave due to the torpedo-set fires."

In addition to the supplies, Kuckens salvaged the ship's compass, sextant, and chronometer. Surviving on raw eggs and small rations of water, the beleaguered crew cast about for ten days before landing at Maui, Hawaii. During the ordeal, four men died of exposure.

Kuckens later served as first mate, then master of several other freighters and Liberty ships. "Dad was an excellent ship handler. He became very skilled from watching schooner captains navigate in dog-hole ports," Ben Kuckens noted. "He favored old style piloting, holding a stopwatch in his hand and a whistle in his mouth."

On May 18, 1957, Capt. Kuckens was backing the Victory ship *P&T Leader* out of a slip in New Haven, Connecticut when he was struck with a fatal heart attack. "During his lifetime, he was aboard twenty-eight different vessels. He was on the bridge where he loved to be," Kuckens said of his father. "He was just like a cowboy, dying in the saddle. He wouldn't have had it any other way."

"Sunny Jim"

On March 3, 1917, the steam schooner *Flavel* was the first vessel to be launched that year on Humboldt Bay. "She slipped quietly into the water early this morning from the Bendixsen yards at Fairhaven," news reports announced. "Owing to the early hour of the ceremony,

Launched in 1917, the steam schooner Flavel *was a "double-ender" which allowed her to carry larger loads of cargo.* San Francisco Maritime National Historical Park.

8:30 o'clock, there were very few present, but among those few, one of the most interested was Mayor James Rolph of San Francisco. He is now negotiating the purchase of the yards that have furnished so many handsome vessels in the Pacific fleet."

Soon after, Rolph concluded his negotiations and added Bendixsen's famous shipbuilding yard to his other business holdings. Born in San Francisco in 1869, James Rolph, Jr. began his entrepreneurial life at fifteen by raising pigeons and selling the meat. He gained an interest in ships after serving as an office boy at a shipping company.

Rolph's long friendship with school classmate George Hind provided a business opportunity in 1898. With capital from Hind's father, a wealthy sugar plantation owner in Hawaii, the two established the Hind, Rolph Shipping Company. The enterprise proved successful and soon was shipping goods up and down the coast as well as abroad.

Rolph succeeded at politics, too. In 1911, he was elected Mayor of San Francisco and served for the next nineteen years. His gregarious, outgoing personality garnered him the nickname of "Sunny Jim." Although gambling and prostitution thrived during his administration, Rolph was seen as "a dapper, man-about-town, with a friendly word for everyone."

Inaugurated as Governor of California in 1930, he faced considerable criticism three years later. Rolph publicly praised citizens of San Jose following the lynching of the confessed murderer Brooke Hart, a local department store heir. His promise to pardon anyone who was part of the vigilante committee earned him the new moniker of "Governor Lynch." Following this episode, he suffered several heart attacks and died before completing his term of office.

Giant Octopus

The *Flavel* was the second of a fleet of four vessels built at the Bendixsen yards for the A.B. Hammond Lumber Company. Named after a town in Oregon where Hammond owned a mill, the new vessel was 210 feet long, 42 feet wide, and measured 967 tons. She was a "double-ender," with a deck both before and aft of the deckhouse which enabled her to carry larger loads of cargo.

Born in Canada in 1848, Andrew B. Hammond left home at age sixteen to work in the logging camps of Maine and Pennsylvania. He drifted to Montana a year later, found employment as a woodcutter and store clerk, and became a partner in a mercantile firm. In the 1880s and

Known for his good humor and publicity stunts, San Francisco Mayor James Rolph, left center in bowler hat, earned the nickname of "Sunny Jim." His business holdings included the noted Bendixsen shipyards where the Flavel *was built.* City of San Francisco.

Timber baron Andrew B. Hammond kept the schooner Flavel *busy hauling lumber from his mills in Oregon and Washington to ports throughout California.* Mansfield Library.

1890s, Hammond expanded his financial holdings by building railroads and assembling huge lumber companies in Oregon and California. He formed the Hammond Lumber Company in 1900. By then, he had moved to San Francisco and established a fleet of steam schooners.

Hammond was a controversial figure who built his career with ruthless determination. Indicted for poaching timber, he managed to avoid prosecution through a series of political maneuverings. Notoriously anti-union, he vigorously opposed collective bargaining, minimum wages, and the eight-hour day. According to one biographer, "He built a lumber empire through his own intelligence and vision and ruled it with an iron hand."

Initially, the *Flavel* made runs to Chile to collect nitrate, an important component of fertilizers. Later, she kept a faithful schedule hauling lumber from the Hammond mills in Oregon and Washington to ports throughout California.

Traveling from Gray's Harbor, Washington to San Pedro, California on December 14, 1923, the *Flavel* was hugging the shore in threatening weather. "Out of the wintry drizzle and through the moaning winds came the dreadful roar of surf pounding upon the shore," writer Henry Rink exclaimed. "Capt. H. Johnson frantically tried to change course. Too late. The strong inflow of the seas pulled the ship like a giant octopus. Shortly after midnight, the big lumber ship struck the promontory of cliffs and rocks just north of Point Pinos."

News of the accident arrived at Monterey in an unusual way. Driving home from an evening dance, H.A. Lyons and his wife heard the hoarse whistle blasts of the stricken ship. As a former Navy man, Lyons recognized them as distress signals. Guided by the sounds, he drove through the woods to the scene of the wreck. After summoning the police, he built a large fire on shore to light the way for survivors and rescue ships.

"Never So Scared"

Upon discovering that the *Flavel*'s hull had split, Capt. Johnson ordered the crew to abandon ship. In the early morning hours, the first lifeboat with twenty-two crew was launched. The men rowed out through the heaviest seas in many months, leaving Capt. Johnson, the first mate, and the chief engineer still aboard. An hour later, the three men decided that further attempts to save the ship were foolhardy and

The Flavel *struck the rocks at Point Pinos in 1923. The captain and crew abandoned the ship after her hull split.* Gene Barron.

fought their way to shore in another boat. Eventually, all were rescued by the Paladini Fish Company's launch *Normandie.*

"I've been at sea all my life. I've been torpedoed and had my share of accidents. But I was never so scared in my life as last night when the *Flavel* was being whipped about in the seas," the chief engineer admitted. "When we went over the side, the old tub rolled toward our little lifeboat, but she rolled back. We paddled our way through the inky blackness with nothing but a little flashlight. We were sure a tired trio when the *Normandie* picked us up."

In the meantime, Capt. John T. Pierce of the Monterey Presidio took a truck with a squad of men to illuminate the scene with searchlights. By this time, in spite of the darkness and rain, a large crowd of people had assembled to view the *Flavel*'s demise. Also brewing was a fight for possession of the *Flavel*. With the ship valued at $50,000 and the million feet of lumber she was carrying at $60,000, four parties joined the fray: the Hammond Lumber Company, the insurance company, Del Monte Properties which owned land where the *Flavel* wrecked, and a band of opportunistic adventurers.

Del Monte Properties announced it would seize the vessel under maritime law. They asserted that the first person aboard any ship abandoned by her master and crew is entitled to full salvage privileges. Capt. Johnson disagreed. Having attempted to re-board the *Flavel*, the skipper said he would turn the vessel over to a representative of the U.S. Marshall's office from San Francisco.

When negotiations were completed, the cargo of lumber was sold to Del Monte. The company sent a force of a hundred men, several tractors, and numerous teams and trucks to salvage the cargo. Lumber was piled mountain-high, along a three mile stretch of beach near Point Pinos.

"Only three days after she crashed onto the rocks, the *Flavel* broke up and completely disappeared," a local newspaper observed. "Her remains, consisting of flotsam and heavy timbers with rusting, twisting bolting, were scattered along the coast."

Battle Scarred

Hailed as "the largest oil tank steamer to fly the American flag," the *Frank H. Buck* was launched February 12, 1914 at the prolific Union Iron Works in San Francisco. The tanker was 408 feet long, 55 feet wide, measured 6,077 tons, and cost over $750,000.

Founded by Irish immigrants Peter and James Donahue in 1849, Union Iron Works became California's premiere producer of mining, railroad, agricultural and locomotive machinery. Between 1884 and 1902, the enterprise also built seventy-five marine vessels, including the first steel hulled ship on the West Coast. In 1905, Bethlehem Shipbuilding Corporation bought the works which operated as part of Bethlehem Steel, producing both warships and merchant ships.

The tanker's launching was significant in another respect. "Her construction set a new record for this type of vessel," the *Coast Seaman's Journal* explained. "The first keel plate was laid on September 6, 1913, five months and four days before she was launched. Since a tanker is divided minutely into compartments with special riveting to retain oil, this record is considered remarkable."

The *Frank H. Buck* was fashioned for Associated Oil, owners of the unlucky *Roderick Dhu*. The vessel had a carrying capacity in excess of 60,000 barrels of oil. She contained eighteen tanks for oil and two cargo pumps capable of discharging the entire cargo in nineteen hours. Initially, she led an uneventful life, puttering between ports up and down the Pacific Coast.

During World War I, she served as an armed auxiliary vessel, carrying oil and supplies from East Coast ports to U.S. forces in France. While in the mid-Atlantic in September of 1918, she took part in a terrific battle with a German submarine, which she sank. Battle scarred, she returned with war honors to resume business in the oil trade.

A Raucous Blast

All remained routine for the *Frank H. Buck* until May 3, 1924. Bound for Monterey, Capt. Sigmund Anderson set a safe course and went below deck, leaving Third Mate George Allen on watch. Having never before been in Monterey Bay, Allen altered the course and went to notify the captain of the change.

In Allen's absence, Seaman A. Visser sighted a landfall on the rocky shore. Assuming he was under orders, he continued on the course. Moments later, traveling at full speed, the vessel careened over two reefs before coming to a shuddering stop. There she sat, cradled precariously on the jagged rocks of Point Pinos.

The ship hit the reefs with a terrific impact, sending a shiver from stem to stern. "On a clear, starry night, the big ship crashed onto a high, dry perch on the tumbled rocks of Point Pinos shore," one report

The tanker Frank H. Buck *careened over two reefs at Point Pinos in 1924. She was repaired and sailed until 1937 when she collided with the passenger ship* President Coolidge *and sank.* Pacific Grove Museum of Natural History.

asserted. "Steel plates screeched and tore apart, rivets popped like dry balls of kelp, men shot free of their bunks."

Immediately, Capt. Anderson ordered the boats lowered. After the lifeboats nearly capsized in the breakers, eighteen of the *Frank H. Buck*'s crew escaped from the ship to the shore. In the chilly night, the saltwater-soaked men huddled miserably around a driftwood fire. The captain stayed aboard with fourteen men, sending seven others ashore in a breeches buoy (a circular lifebuoy, attached to a pair of rubber pants, used to extract people from wrecked vessels).

"The following day, hot dog stands and ice cream kiosks burgeoned forth around the point and crowds poured forth to view the ill-fated ship," a local newspaper reported. "The owners appeared on the scene and the bow was pushed high above the rocks with hydraulic jacks. Large buoys were placed offshore and heavy cables were secured to the ship's stern."

Fortunately, the tanker was empty when she grounded. On May 17th, the ship was freed from the reef and re-floated at high tide with the assistance of the steam schooners *Peacock* and *Homer*. A crowd of over 2,000 people witnessed the event. In a prolonged and raucous blast of triumph, the throng cheered and honked automobile horns as the *Frank H. Buck* slid into the sea. From there, she was towed to San Francisco for repairs.

Drawing A Curtain

Twelve more years passed quietly for the great tanker. Then, on March 6, 1937, she collided in the fog with the passenger ship *President Coolidge* in San Francisco Bay. The liner was owned by Robert Dollar. After dropping out of school and laboring at menial jobs, Dollar became known internationally as a lumber baron, shipping magnate, and philanthropist. California Governor James Rolph noted, "Robert Dollar has done more to spread the American flag on the high seas than any man in this country."

The impact tore a huge hole in the eight million dollar liner. Nearly seven hundred passengers wandered anxiously around the ship, wondering whether they could resume their voyage to Hawaii and the Orient. The *Frank H. Buck* began sinking immediately. The crew took to the lifeboats and was quickly picked up by the *President Coolidge*. With the tanker carrying 67,000 barrels of oil, it was considered a miracle

A breeches buoy like this one was used to extract crew members from the Frank H. Buck *when she stranded at Point Pinos.* United States Coast Guard.

With damaged bow the President Coolidge *returns to port for repairs before continuing on her voyage.* Michael McFadyen.

that she didn't erupt in flames. Experts agreed, "Had the crash not been particularly bow on, an explosion could easily have occurred."

As the damaged luxury liner returned to the San Francisco wharf, her band played "Whistling in the Dark." Meanwhile, a dozen rescue craft sped to the wreck scene. Although it seemed that she would go down at any moment, the indomitable tanker held on. According to the *San Francisco Chronicle*, "Doggedly, she fumbled her way through the banks of fog and finally sank her nose in a mud bank a hundred yards off shore where she held fast during the night."

The fact that she was full of oil was believed to be a factor keeping her afloat so long. Salvage vessels moved in and began pumping the first of 4,600 barrels of oil and water from the *Frank H. Buck*'s tanks. High above the scene, a maze of traffic and curious onlookers crept along the overhanging bluffs.

Lashed by surf and heavy swells, the *Frank H. Buck*'s inevitable end arrived. She came to rest near her sister ship, the *Lyman Stewart*, which suffered a similar fate in 1922. The twin tankers had been built on adjacent ways in San Francisco and launched in 1914 within a few days of each other.

A comment by Capt. Karl A. Ahlin of the *President Coolidge* seemed an appropriate obituary for the *Frank H. Buck*. "Fog is one of those things we will never be able to control," he reflected. "The accident was one of those things that is over before you can see it, like drawing a curtain across a window."

9

WANDERLUST

February 23, 1933

After starting out life in the Cape Horn grain trade, the *William H. Smith* was destined to live long, plying the seas for five decades. She was virtually a chameleon, mutating from a full-rigged sailing ship, to a floating cannery, a coal barge, and finally a five-masted cargo schooner. A kaleidoscope of renowned ship owners and ship masters steered her through a memorable and ultimately tragic career.

Durable Down Easter

As the hub of American shipping, Bath, Maine produced some of the most durable and elegant ships to ever sail. Among them, was the Down Easter *William H. Smith*. According to one account, "She was fashioned of sturdy northern pine and constructed to withstand the pounding of mountainous seas. Much of her interior was finished in Spanish walnut, mahogany, teak, and oak."

By the mid-nineteenth century, Bath was the nation's fifth largest seaport, creating clipper ships that sailed to ports around the globe. Production of these quick, hardy, dependable vessels soared. Roughly five thousand ships were launched in the area, which at one time boasted more than two hundred shipbuilding firms.

The noted shipbuilding firm of Goss, Sawyer & Packard, was established in 1873 at Bath, Maine. Many durable and elegant Down Easters were constructed here, including the William H. Smith *in 1883.* Patten Free Library.

"Along the Maine Coast, people are born with salt in their blood," author William H. Rowe asserted. "At Bath the stocks producing great ships that carried cargos to the ends of the earth crowded one upon the next along the shore. More ships have been built on that strip of Bath shore front than any other of equal area in the world."

After the Civil War, large wooden sailing ships called "Down Easters" were built in Massachusetts and Maine almost exclusively, with Bath as the capital of the activity. The term Down Easter arose from the fact that when ships sailed from Boston to ports in Maine, which was to the east of Boston, the wind was at their backs. They were sailing downwind, hence "Down East."

Although Down Easters like the *William H. Smith* maintained the fast, sleek lines of clipper ships, they were deeper and fuller in shape. This meant they could carry as much as one-and-a-half times the cargo as the average clipper. These vessels rarely came back to Bath, but ran between major seaports of the world making money for the owners carrying products such as grain, coal, hemp, jute, hides, iron rails, sugar, and wool.

An Enviable Record

The *William H. Smith* was constructed in 1883 by the prominent firm of Goss, Sawyer & Packard. The driving force behind the enterprise was Capt. Guy C. Goss. Born in Maine in 1823, he was first a school teacher, then a shipmaster, and finally a shipbuilder. One biographer noted, "He followed the sea for twenty-five years, then engaged in shipbuilding for twenty-five more, making half a century of connection with ships and the ocean."

During the Civil War, the United States had lost much of its shipping to attacks by Confederate cruisers and by sales of ships to other countries. In addition, the cost of materials continued to increase. Many ship owners and shipbuilders were disheartened about the outlook of rebuilding the nation's merchant fleet. Most thought it would be impossible to restore American shipping to what it was before the war.

"Capt. Goss believed it was the duty of every citizen to do all that he could to build up what the war had torn down. He remarked to those who said we were ruined, that it was better to fail trying to do something than to lie down and make no effort," one colleague observed. "If we did not build ships, other nations would. Capt. Goss and his partners did what they could to awaken an interest in our shipping."

Capt. Guy C. Goss, the founder of Goss, Sawyer & Packard, was a prominent shipmaster and shipbuilder. International Maritime Exhibition.

Having successfully built his first schooner in 1865, Capt. Goss formed the partnership of Goss & Sawyer in 1866 with Elijah F. Sawyer. In 1873, Benjamin F. Packard was added to the enterprise which became known as Goss, Sawyer & Packard. Both Sawyer and Packard were well known shipwrights. "They were two as good mechanics as there were in the country," an admirer commented. "They were brought up in the school of such master builders as William Webb, John English, Paul Curtis, and Donald McKay who had made a world wide reputation from ships."

The business increased until 1884 when it was put into the hands of the New England Shipbuilding Company with Capt. Goss as president. Sadly, Packard died the following year. Capt. Goss resigned in 1888 and passed away in May 1890. New England Shipbuilding reorganized, forming an offshoot called Kelley-Spear Company. Sawyer headed the firm until he passed away in September 1906. In the forty years of their existence, the combined companies produced an enviable record of 315 vessels which included some of the finest schooners, steamers, and Down Easters ever made.

Raiders and Traders

In the first three years of the 1880s, the building of Down Easters boomed. This was due largely to the West Coast's bumper wheat harvest of 1882 which brought increased prosperity to grain carriers. One historian explained, "California could produce wheat so hard and dry that it could stand the 14,000 mile voyage around Cape Horn and arrive in European ports in prime condition."

Among those hoping to make a profit were the brothers F.H. and William H. Smith. Based in New York, they ordered construction of the *William H. Smith* for their firm of F.H. Smith & Company. The vessel was 232 feet long, 43 feet wide, and measured 1,957 tons. Although the Smiths' principal interests were in schooners and barkentines, the time seemed right to expand. Subsequently, they operated steamers in the coastwise trade in the Atlantic but were only mildly successful.

The two brothers chose Capt. J.F. Bartlett as the *William H. Smith*'s first master. Seven years later, Capt. Rowland Bridgham Brown was signed on and stayed in command for ten years. Born in 1840, he was a native of Castine, Maine, one of the oldest towns in New England. He went to sea at age twelve as a Grand Banks fisherman in Newfoundland.

Capt. Rowland B. Brown commanded the William H. Smith *for ten years. His gravesite is in Castine, Maine, one of the oldest towns in New England.* Castine Cemetery.

Filled with Atlantic cod, swordfish, haddock, scallops, and lobster, Grand Banks is among the richest fishing grounds in the world.

During the Civil War, Brown studied navigation, enlisted in the U.S. Navy, and was appointed an Ensign. He served with the North Atlantic Blockading Squadron, cutting off Confederate supply routes, and with the West India Squadron, seeking out and destroying Confederate raiders. After the war, Brown resigned from the Navy to re-enter the merchant marine. From 1867 to 1900 he was accompanied on nearly all of his voyages by his wife Margaret and their five children. Capt. Brown retired from sea life in 1900. He passed away in 1920, having spent his remaining years at his home in Castine, Maine.

Faced with increasing financial difficulties, F.H. Smith & Company was forced to liquidate most of their business holdings in 1892. They clung to the *William H. Smith* until 1900 when she was sold to the California Shipping Company of San Francisco. Organized by William E. Mighell in 1899, the enterprise was incorporated with a million dollars in capital and backed by over thirty prominent investors. The entrepreneurs collected a vast fleet of ships that shuffled in and out of San Francisco carrying goods and passengers to ports up and down the Pacific Coast.

In 1911, the *William H. Smith* was purchased by the Weiding & Independent Fisheries Company of Seattle, Washington. According to one maritime historian, "The vessel had reverted to a barge status. More than a year before she had lost a bout with a rollicking storm off Cape Flattery, Washington. She was purchased as she lay in her storm-battered condition."

Andrew Weiding, a Norwegian immigrant and captain of fishing vessels, converted the ship into a floating cannery for the Alaska fishing trade. Like others of its kind, the *William H. Smith* contained quarters for crew as well as facilities for receiving, dressing, and cleaning the fish which were brought aboard by means of a portable elevator attached to the side of the ship. The vessel also served as a cold storage plant with equipment for cooling, freezing, and storing the pack.

Six years later, the *William H. Smith* changed hands, and duties, again. This time, she was purchased by the Pacific Coast Coal Company for use as a coal barge. The firm was part of the rail, shipping and coal operations formed under the Pacific Coast Company. Formed in late 1897, it comprised several existing organizations, most notably the Pacific Coast Steamship Company, Pacific Coast Coal Company, and the Pacific Coast Railway.

The William H. Smith *was converted into a floating cannery in 1911 for the Alaska fishing trade. A portable elevator was attached to the side of the ship for loading the catch.* University of Washington Libraries.

The Pacific Coast Coal Company purchased the
William H. Smith in 1917 for use as a coal barge.
Museum of History & Industry

The companies served the West Coast from the mid-nineteenth century until its last railways were abandoned or sold in the mid-twentieth century.

"Iron Man of the Sea"

Faced with another transition, the *William H. Smith*'s wanderlust continued. In July 1919, she was sold to Charles Nelson & Company, a firm created by Danish immigrant Charles Nelson. Like so many others seeking their fortune, Nelson was attracted to San Francisco in 1850 by news of gold discoveries. Meeting with only fair success at mining, he secured an interest in a whaling boat at Sacramento. With the assistance of a comrade, he rowed the whaler from Sacramento to Marysville, a distance of ninety miles, carrying freight and passengers. He made the trip frequently, often buying vegetables and garden produce, which were sold in the city.

As his financial resources increased, Nelson invested in vessels of his own and by 1900 had developed a large lumber shipping business. Trade extended to China, South America, and Australia. Capt. Nelson continued to oversee his immense shipping interests until a short time before his death in 1909 at age seventy-nine.

Having purchased the *William H. Smith*, Nelson's successors re-rigged the vessel as a five-masted schooner for carrying lumber and other cargo. One of the men who served aboard the ship during voyages to Australia in 1923 and 1924 was Chief Mate Charles J. Tulee. Born in 1891, Tulee went to sea at age fifteen as a cabin boy on a German ship. He sailed to San Francisco in 1911 on a ship from the Netherlands and later served on other notable vessels including the clipper ship *Falls of Clyde* and the World War I steamship *Ohioan*. He was also aboard the wooden passenger steamer *San Juan* when she wrecked near Pigeon Point Lighthouse.

Traveling from San Francisco to San Pedro at midnight on August 29, 1929, the vessel was struck by a tanker twice her size and sank within five minutes. Seventy-five men, women, and children perished in the disaster. It was the area's worst maritime tragedy.

Tulee, the *San Juan*'s first officer, was off duty. "I was in my room on the bridge deck. The blowing of the fog whistle kept me awake," he recalled. "When I heard the *San Juan* and a nearby steamer each blow three blasts, I ran on deck knowing that a collision might occur. I was

Charles J. Tulee, pictured with his wife Ellen, was chief mate of the William H. Smith *during voyages to Australia in 1923 and 1924.* Roy Tulee.

on the main deck when the crash came. A minute and a half later my feet were in the water."

One of the few survivors, Tulee was picked up by a boat from the tanker. Although overwrought at the loss of the *San Juan*, Tulee provided a clear account of the aftermath of the collision. "I was not near the lifeboats and do not know whether any were lowered. I heard no signal to the crew to go to their stations," he revealed. "It all happened so suddenly. There was not more than ninety seconds from the crash to the sinking. There was no time to lower the boats or put on life preservers."

Numbed by his brush with death, Tulee recovered sufficiently to go back to sea as master of both sailing vessels and steamships. In 1942, as master of the wooden schooner *Commodore*, Capt. Tulee was bound from Port Angeles, Washington to Durban, South Africa with a load of redwood. During the 143-day voyage he became ill and died. His colorful career earned him the title of "Iron Man of the Sea." According to one biographer, "Capt. Tulee had faced death many times in howling gales and mountainous seas and always was the bravest man aboard his ship."

Last Brief Cruise

The *William H. Smith* remained active until 1927, often towed by steam schooners along the coast and sometimes making voyages under sail to Hawaii or Mexico. She was laid up at Oakland until 1932 when she was sold to "old time Monteryan" Horace Cochran. He was proprietor of the Monterey Boat Works where commercial fishing boats were built and repaired, and where rumrunners frequently landed during prohibition. Cochran was described by the *Monterey County Herald* as "an entrepreneur of many interests, most relating to maritime activities."

Unfortunately, the sailing days of the *William H. Smith* were numbered. At dusk on February 23, 1933, a fifty mile per hour gale whipped Monterey Bay into a froth of whitecaps. The vessel's anchor chain snapped, pitching her onto a rocky reef. By the following morning, her five masts had splintered and her hull was breaking up before the smashing waves.

Tragedy nearly marked the end of the old craft. The ship's watchman, twenty-three year-old Edwin Berglund, was aboard when she broke adrift. Knowing the danger of leaving the ship in the dark, he spent the

Re-rigged as a five-masted schooner, the William H. Smith *grounded north of Point Pinos in 1933.* Pacific Grove Museum of Natural History.

night rolling about in the breakers. Stiff and weary, Berglund survived the night, but had a narrow escape the next morning. Making his way to shore hand-over-hand, he lost his grip on a life-line and fell ten feet short of the rescue ship.

"The water was already strewn with wreckage and Berglund, unable to swim, was in danger when he lost hold of the rope," a local newspaper reported. "Once again it was drawn taut and the watchman made his way to shore, none the worse for his experience, aside from a dunking and sleepless night."

Hundreds of people gathered along the beach as the *William H. Smith* broke up under the relentless beating of the surf. Piles of wreckage were strewn along a wide section of the shore and scores of men and women searched excitedly for bronze bolts or fittings that might serve as souvenirs.

In an attempt to salvage the ship, which was loaded with wood, Cochran sent a truck, tractor, and rescue team to the scene. Although it seemed unlikely that she could be saved, a crew of more than twenty men busied themselves stacking timbers on the beach and loading them onto the trucks. Cochran kept a watch on the beach throughout the day, hoping the ship's ornate cabin would wash ashore.

"Fate decreed an inglorious end for the old ship, one of the few remaining relics of the days when white winged barques were the backbone of world commerce," the *Monterey Herald* lamented. "Unlike many of her sister ships whose careers were climaxed spectacularly on rocky reefs during furious storms in far off places, the *William H. Smith* merely gave a heavy lunge, broke her anchor chain, and set out for her last brief cruise."

10

Rum Chaser

September 25, 1933

The Coast Guard patrol boat *CG-256* experienced the adventure of chasing rum runners as well as the more serene duty of observing the strikes of sardine fishermen. Her short career came to a halt on a sharp snag-toothed rock at Point Pinos.

Prohibition Era

The practice of smuggling liquor is as old as the substance itself. In the 1500s, the British government operated revenue cutters to stop smugglers. Pirates created lucrative enterprises running rum to heavily taxed colonies. As early as 1600, nautical terms appeared to describe a state of inebriation, including "listing to starboard," "three sheets to the wind," "carrying too much sail," and "decks awash."

By far the most famous period of rum running occurred in the United States between 1920 and 1933. The passing of the Eighteenth Amendment prohibited the sale, possession, and consumption of alcohol. It proved to be an extremely unpopular law. Reveling in an otherwise liberated era, many citizens enjoyed a good stiff drink now and again, even if it was illegal.

A quote by Eleanor Roosevelt captures the essence of the times: "Little by little it dawned upon me that this law was not making people drink any less, but it was making hypocrites and law breakers of a great number of people."

Technically, it was never illegal to drink during Prohibition. The Eighteenth Amendment and the Volstead Act, the legal measure that included the instructions for enforcing Prohibition, never barred the consumption of alcohol, just making it, selling it, and shipping it for mass production. Private ownership and consumption of alcohol was not made illegal under federal law, but in some areas, local laws were quite strict.

The introduction of alcohol prohibition was a hotly-debated issue. Prohibition supporters, called "drys," presented it as a victory for public morals and health. Anti-prohibitionists, known as "wets," criticized the alcohol ban as an intrusion of rural ideals on urban life. Prohibition also created a criminal underground as well as an unprecedented flow of liquor from the sea.

"The Real McCoy"

The first few months of Prohibition were deceptively quiet along America's shores. One of the earliest official references to the growing illicit trade was in the Coast Guard's 1921 annual report. The Florida coast patrol was cited as "particularly vigilant, having made hundreds of trips to support Prohibition authorities and seize vessels."

A Florida boat builder and excursion boat captain named Bill McCoy, who became the self-styled "King of the Rum Runners," set the pattern for smuggling liquor by sea. He brought ships to the edge of the three mile limit of U.S. jurisdiction and sold his wares to "contact boats" owned by local fishermen and small boat captains. McCoy was famous for never watering his booze, and selling only top-of-the-line name brands. Reputedly, this was the origin of the term "The Real McCoy," meaning genuine and on the level.

During his career, McCoy made hundreds of thousands of dollars and personally delivered more than 700,000 cases of liquor to U.S. shores. In his autobiography, he explained what drew him into this illegal trade. "I went into rum running for the cash. There was money in the game, lots if you could keep it," he wrote. "Beyond that there was all the kick of gambling and the thrill of sport. There was open sea and the boom

The Prohibition Era of 1920 to 1933 created an unprecedented flow of liquor furnished by rum runners. Authorities confiscated hundreds of cases of illegal booze from each ship. Metro Jacksonville.

of the wind against full sails, dawn coming out of the ocean, and nights under rocking stars. These caught and held me most of all."

The three mile limit became known as the "Rum Line," and vessels waiting to receive illegal spirits were called "Rum Row." In 1924, the Rum Line was extended to a twelve mile limit, making it more difficult for smaller and less seaworthy craft to travel the distance. With the run to shore longer, chances of detection increased. In a desperate attempt to avoid arrest, some rum runners dumped their cargo, set the vessel on fire, and abandoned ship.

Often, crews armed themselves against government ships and against other rum runners. Some rum boats sank others to hijack precious cargo, rather than journey to Canada or Mexico to restock their liquid supplies. At night, even in fog, they often ran at high speeds and without lights. Many smashed into rocks, spilling their profits overboard.

Ironically, one thing that rum runners seldom carried was rum. The name was a holdover from the rum smuggling of colonial days, and from the habit of referring to all liquor as the "demon rum." Most of the cargo was whiskey bottled in Canada and Mexico by professional distillers.

After California voted to join other dry states, rum runners flocked to its shores. Secluded coves along the coastline became ideal locations for their illegal operations. Newspapers of the era are filled with accounts of coastal prohibition squads searching for huge caches of smuggled liquor.

Rum War

The task of pursuing rum runners was assigned to the U.S. Coast Guard, a small arm of the Treasury Department. When Prohibition began in 1920, the service was ill-equipped to cope with zealous lawbreakers. Thousands of miles of coast had to be patrolled by a fleet of less than a hundred ships and a meager workforce of 4,000. Some reports indicate that no more than five percent of the U.S. bound liquor was stopped between 1920 and 1925.

Nicknamed "Carry Nation's Navy" after the hatchet-swinging temperance leader, Coast Guard vessels consisted of an assortment of cruising cutters, inshore patrol boats, and harbor cutters. As the rum tide continued to rise in epidemic proportions, pressure built to develop a fleet designed to meet the growing problem.

Chased by Coast Guard patrol boats, some rum runners set their ships afire to destroy evidence of their contraband. United States Coast Guard.

Like the CG-256, *this "six-bitter" patrol boat chased rum runners during the Prohibition Era.* United States Coast Guard.

During 1925, Coast Guard personnel increased to over ten thousand. The largest single element of the expansion was the construction of over two hundred new patrol boats. Twenty-five of the ships were built on the West Coast. These sturdy seventy-five foot vessels, known as "six-bitters," became the mainstay of the Rum War. The nickname came from the colloquial term of "six bits," meaning seventy-five cents.

Built at Alameda, California by A.W. DeYoung, the *CG-256* entered the water in 1925 as one of the Coast Guard's new rum chasers. Designed for seventeen knots and a crew of eight, the patrol boat emphasized seaworthiness and endurance over speed. Intended for offshore work, the vessel picketed rum ships beyond the twelve mile limit to prevent contact boats from obtaining their loads of liquor. She was armed with machine guns and a one-pound rapid fire gun. Aiding a more aggressive stance toward rum runners were new agreements with other maritime nations which allowed the Coast Guard to patrol twenty to thirty miles at sea.

The newly-minted *CG-256* was nearly lost before her rum chasing days began. During an early morning run on January 9, 1925, she collided in dense fog with the ferry steamer *Cazadero* near San Francisco's Alcatraz Island. According to the patrol boat's skipper, G.H. Jacobsen, a member of his crew was thrown overboard by the impact. Following an anxiety-filled search of twenty minutes, he was sighted and picked up by a small boat from the *Cazadero*. "The fog was one of the heaviest that has visited the bay region in known history," a local newspaper reported. "The ferry suffered damage to one of her paddle wheels. The *CG-256* was damaged considerably but remained afloat."

Prohibition, along with rum running, ended in December 1933. Between 1925 and the close of Prohibition, the Coast Guard seized nearly five hundred rum ships. "The fight against liquor smuggling is one of the most complex naval operations ever executed," Rear Admiral Frederick C. Billard asserted. "The Coast Guard was given the task and it did not discuss it or argue about it. It simply answered, 'Aye, Aye, Sir,' and sailed into the job."

Sardine Capital of the World

With the Prohibition Era winding down, the *CG-256* was given other patrol duties. In September of 1933, her assignment in Monterey was cited as "observation duty in connection with the strike of sardine fishermen." At the time, Monterey carried the reputation of the "sardine capital of the world."

Known for its vast offshore harvest of salmon and sardines, the waters off Monterey were, and still are, popular fishing grounds. Although a fisherman's luck was always precarious, fishing vessels called purse seiners resulted in a larger catch. Their nets, which operated much like the drawstrings of an old-fashioned purse, were heavier, more efficient, and could snare more fish. Many fishermen offered up their own version of a prayer by muttering, "May the holes in your net be no larger than the fish in it."

Finding shoals of fish at night requires far more than fisherman's luck. On moonless nights, it took experience and skill to spot the "green flash" of schooling sardines. And, the arduous task of deploying an unwieldy net off a moving boat on the open sea in total darkness took teamwork and courage.

Traditionally, sardines, also called pilchard, were canned "wet from the sea" with little pre-processing. Because of this, they were dubbed "wetfish." Sardine fishermen, hauling their catch aboard using huge purse seine nets, were drenched in a shower of seawater, giving the term a double meaning. The work was both soggy and cumbersome.

Sardines were off-loaded into buckets five hundred pounds at a time, and hoisted by cable to the canneries. The pilchard were measured and weighed, then sent to cutting sheds. In the early 1930s, the bucket and cable method was replaced by a system of floating wooden pens, or "hoppers," anchored safely out from Monterey Bay's dangerous reefs. Hoppers were connected to the canneries by large pipe-like underwater hoses, employing massive pumps to literally suck the sardines ashore for processing.

Wartime Bonanza

Originally, the grueling work of preparing and packing sardine tins along Monterey's "Cannery Row" was almost exclusively done by women. Often before dawn, a chorus of cannery whistles, each with its own pitch and pattern, called workers to the lines and warehouses. Cutting, packing, and cooking continued until that night's catch was canned, no matter how long it took.

"Cannery Row is a poem, a stink, a grating noise, a quality of light, a tone, a habit, a nostalgia, a dream," novelist John Steinbeck wrote.

Author John Steinbeck wrote about Monterey's Cannery Row when it was the "sardine capital of the world." Author's Collection.

"Cannery Row is the gathered and scattered, chipped pavement and weedy lots and junk heaps, and sardine canneries of corrugated iron."

Sardines were cut by hand, drained, and dried on wooden slats or "flakes." Large flat metal baskets of flaked fish were drawn through long troughs of boiling peanut oil, drained again, packed into cans, and hand soldered closed. Labeling and boxing for warehousing and shipment completed the operation. These canning processes prevailed until World War I when canneries were mechanized.

During the war, the sardine industry surged. Orders for non-perishable canned fish poured in from both civilian and military buyers. Cannery Row's wartime sardine production grew from 75,000 cases in 1915 to 1.4 million cases in 1918. Similarly, the price per case rose from $2.14 to $7.50. Eventually, Cannery Row housed over twenty sardine processing plants.

The wartime bonanza was, of course, too good to last. The end of World War I, and its ensuing recession, saw a scramble for survival by the sardine factories along Cannery Row. Reduction of sardines into fertilizer and fish meal, once a profitable sideline to canning, became a separate and dominant industry.

The period of depression was softened by the general success of Monterey's sardine industry. As the sardine fleet and the canning capacity expanded, an average catch of over 100,000 tons per season was recorded through the 1930s. The industry reached its peak in 1934, yielding over 230,000 tons of sardines. The trend continued during World War II, with the catch averaging over 200,000 tons per season. Pacific sardines accounted for one fourth of all the fish landed in the United States.

Sent Heavenward

Struggling through pea-soup fog at midnight on September 25, 1933, the Coast Guard patrol boat *CG-256* hit a sharp snag-toothed rock off Point Pinos. Although the captain and crew attempted to free the ship from the rocks, the engines lost power and water sloshed through a hole in the hull. The skipper, Chief Boatswain's Mate M.E. Nichol ordered his crew to the lifeboat.

In launching the dory, Nichol's foot caught in a rope, slamming him against the side of the ship. Five shipmates leaped to his rescue. The slightly bruised and battered band landed safely on a rock near the beach. Several of the crew waded into the water to follow the shoreline

Point Pinos Lighthouse Keeper Peter C. Nelson and his wife Ida Pate Nelson provided hot coffee and warm clothing to the CG-256's *shipwrecked crew.* Pacific Grove Museum of Natural History.

to Point Pinos lighthouse while the skipper stood by his ship. "At the lighthouse, they were given hot coffee," one report said. "Their clothing was dried and some extra wraps provided."

Greeting the saturated sailors were Keeper Peter C. Nelson and his wife, Ida. Nelson began his career as third assistant keeper at Point Sur in 1892. While stationed there, he married Ida Pate, a member of a well-known Big Sur family. The couple had two children, both of whom were born at the lighthouse.

Prior to their arrival at Point Pinos in 1931, the Nelsons gained a good deal of experience with maritime disasters. In 1894, they turned Point Sur Lighthouse into a make-shift hospital for survivors of the wrecked steamship *Los Angeles*. The vessel struck a submerged pinnacle of rocks seven hundred yards west of the lighthouse. The impact sent passengers and crew thrashing around in the surf. Six people perished in the tragedy. According to survivors, "The folks there treated us handsomely and furnished well-cooked food, dry clothing, and stimulants."

In 1902, duties took the Nelsons to Ballast Point Lighthouse in San Diego, then on to Lime Point Lighthouse in San Francisco. At Lime Point, they witnessed the wreck of the steamship *Alameda* in 1905. Enveloped by fog while sailing through the Golden Gate, the vessel went hard and fast on the rocks. Water flooded the engine room through a hole perforating the hull. In this instance, all passengers and crew were unharmed.

Upon his retirement in January 1938, Nelson was one of the four longest serving lighthouse keepers in the United States and the most senior keeper on the Pacific Coast. When he passed away in 1964, newspapers noted, "He was a Peninsula pioneer and well-known lighthouse keeper."

The *CG-262* and the *C.G. McClellan* were sent from San Francisco to assist in salvaging the *CG-256*'s light cannon, machine guns, rifles, searchlight, and assorted instruments. Crowds lined the shoreline, perched on points of rock. They watched breathlessly as the salvaging crew ran lines out to the pinioned vessel in an attempt to board her.

"When they got the lines on her and started ashore in the dory in heavy seas that crashed over and around them, the women on the beach let out scream after scream," The *Monterey Trader* exclaimed. "The dory would go straight down over the first line of breakers, then the second line would hit, and everybody thought they were gone."

During his career, Keeper Peter C. Nelson witnessed more than one shipwreck. Here he testifies at a hearing following the wreck of the steamship Alameda *in San Francisco.* San Francisco Call.

The salvaging crew survived, finished their work, and abandoned the little patrol boat. According to one report, "All that remained of the *CG-256* was sent heavenward in the sparks of a funeral pyre."

The Coast Guard patrol boat CG-256 *hit a sharp rock off Point Pinos and sank in 1935. The crew survived, along with some of the ship's artillery and instruments.* Robert Schwemmer.

11

DESPERATION AND DOOM

September 3, 1934

The schooner *J.B. Stetson* was a familiar sight in Pacific Coast ports for nearly three decades. She sailed on despite the death of a captain on her deck, the suicide of one of her owners, shattering storms, and collisions with other vessels. Her final fight with the sea came on the wave-lashed shores of Point Pinos.

Grace and Speed

Isaac, Winslow, and Henry Knox Hall came from a long line of shipwrights, caulkers, riggers, and seafaring men. During the 1840s, the trio acquired expertise at the center of America's boatbuilding industry in Cohasset, Massachusetts. Located near Boston, Cohasset developed into an important port through its shipbuilding, trading, and fishing industries.

The Halls launched their first West Coast vessel at San Francisco in 1863. By 1870, the city had expanded into the tenth largest in the nation, increasing the profitability of shipbuilding. The Pacific Northwest offered promising opportunities, too, with timber operations and sawmills popping up throughout the region. Recognizing the potential for enlarging their shipbuilding enterprise, the brothers relocated to

The lumber schooner J.B. Stetson *was built in 1905 at Winslow, Washington by the noted Hall Brothers Shipyard. She was a familiar sight in Pacific Coast ports for nearly three decades.* William Phelps.

Port Ludlow in 1874, formalizing their business partnership as the Hall Brothers Shipyard.

In 1881, the brothers moved their facilities south to Port Blakely on the east side of Bainbridge Island. The port's sheltered harbor and deep water made it an ideal location for sawmills and shipbuilding. The Halls opened operations next to the flourishing Port Blakely Mill which employed 1,200 men and cut 400,000 feet of timber a day. The mill sprouted into the largest sawmill in the world, shipping lumber to California, Australia, England, Germany, France, South America, and the eastern United States.

The Hall shipyard was transferred to Madrone on Eagle Harbor, north of Port Blakely in 1902. Appropriately, the town was renamed Winslow. Over their long career, the Hall Brothers constructed 108 wooden sailing ships for merchants in the Northwest, San Francisco, and Hawaii. According to an admirer, "Hall Brothers vessels were distinguished by exceptional workmanship, exquisite hull lines, long sharp bows, graceful sterns, great speed, large capacity, and ease of sailing."

One of these fine ships was the *Cornell*. Built at Winslow in 1905, the steam schooner was 181 feet long, 39 feet wide, measured 837 tons, and was valued at $25,000. Commissioned by San Francisco businessman William Gissler, Jr., he sold the newly finished vessel to his acquaintance Ira J. Harmon who renamed her *J.B. Stetson*.

Best, Worst, and Last

When Capt. Samuel Bonifield strode aboard the *J.B. Stetson*, he claimed the schooner as his own. The captain would spend some of his best and worst days, as well as his last days, on the deck of this worthy little ship.

Born in 1850, Bonifield moved with his family from Ohio to San Francisco when he was ten years old. He would later become identified with ships plying the coast for forty years. In the early days, he skippered the schooners *Jessie Nickerson*, *Iaqua*, and *Farallon*.

His most notable command was the steamship *Humboldt* which he helped to build. When the gold rush to Alaska began in 1896, she was crowded with prospectors and fortune hunters stampeding into the territory. "The steamship *Humboldt* sailed with 320 passengers and 800 tons of cargo," the *Seattle Post-Intelligencer* reported of one voyage.

Capt. Samuel Bonifield was the J.B. Stetson's *first master. He died on the schooner's bridge in 1911.* San Francisco Chronicle.

The steamship Humboldt *was Capt. Samuel Bonifield's most notable command. During the gold rush to Alaska in 1896, she was crowded with prospectors stampeding into the territory.* University of Washington Libraries.

"Not an unoccupied berth or an inch of space for freight remained on the ship."

While in command of the steamship *Valencia* in 1902, Capt. Bonifield received a gold medal from the officers and men of the Twenty-Sixth and Ninety-Fourth Coast Artillery Corps for saving the lives of fifteen men from the two companies who went adrift in a small boat off the coast of Alaska. The corps was responsible for coastal and harbor defense of the United States between 1901 and 1950.

Capt. Bonifield was master of the *Northland* when she suffered a mishap at Point Pinos on her maiden voyage in 1904. Less than two years later, he had another rough start as the *J.B Stetson*'s first skipper. On June 12, 1906, the schooner collided with the four-masted barkentine *Jane L. Stanford* off the coast of Washington. Built for the lumber trade, the 970 ton ship traveled in style throughout the Pacific, also visiting the shores of Hawaii, Australia, Chile, and China. "The vessel presented a beautiful appearance. She is painted dark green on the outside to the waterline, below which she is copper painted," one description said. "The cabins are elegantly finished in maple, walnut, and oak."

The collision resulted in the *Jane L. Stanford* losing her bowsprit, one of her masts, and part of her stern, while the *J.B. Stetson* escaped practically unharmed. Capt. Bonifield's license was suspended for a year for "lack of skill and negligence in handling his ship." However, since he was not on deck at the time of the collision, the skipper was exonerated later of the charges. Despite the decision, Supervising Inspector John Bermingham blamed the captain for "not slowing up after the collision for the purpose of ascertaining how badly the *Jane L. Stanford* was damaged."

Fortunately, Capt. Bonifield's reputation remained intact and he stayed at the schooner's helm until March 25, 1911. While the *J.B. Stetson* lay in San Pedro Harbor, the skipper was taken ill with pneumonia. Despite the urging of the ship's officers, he refused to be taken to the hospital, insisted on remaining on his ship, and ordered that she proceed to San Francisco at the scheduled time.

Once underway, Capt. Bonifield took a brief rest below then started for the bridge. Although his officers saw that he was suffering from delirium, they could not prevail upon him to return to his cabin. A scuffle ensued, but being a large man who was much heavier than either of his officers, the skipper successfully pushed through them. He lurched to the bridge, only to collapse. One newspaper noted, "Captain Bonifield was a brave man, unswerving in his trust and devotion to duty."

Desperate Action

Following Capt. Bonifield's demise, the *J.B. Stetson* was sold to the Hicks-Haupman Lumber Company. Headquartered in San Francisco, business partners Earl S. Hicks and Sidney H. Hauptman operated five lumber schooners along the Pacific Coast.

While under their ownership, the *J.B. Stetson* made the headlines again. This time, it was for making a monumental rescue of the historic schooner *C.A. Thayer*. After the vessel sprang a leak off the Washington coast in January 1912 only the half-million feet of lumber and the constant work of eight men at the ship's pumps kept her afloat.

In command of the *C.A. Thayer* was Capt. Carroll Scott, accompanied by his plucky young wife. "She cheered us up every hour, and she kept us going on coffee and bread. We'd 'a quit and gone down if it hadn't been for her," one of the sailors remarked. "One night she sang to us, and she stood next to the captain while he was at the wheel and sang to him. She carried us through, and kept up heart."

The *C.A. Thayer*'s crew passed several nights wet, hungry, and tired, on a waterlogged ship drifting toward shore. Each morning the fog failed to lift. Finally, they heard the tooting of a ship's whistle. It belonged to the *J. B. Stetson* which sent over a tow line and a relief crew, giving the *C.A. Thayer*'s weary men their first rest in a week. The *J.B. Stetson* went on with her duties, towing the saturated schooner and crew nearly 500 miles to San Francisco. The *C.A. Thayer* is on display at the San Francisco Maritime National Historic Park as the last commercial sailing vessel to operate on the West Coast.

In September 1913, the Hicks-Haupman Lumber Company ceased operation when Earl Hicks committed suicide by shooting himself in the head at home. Ill health and business struggles due to a recent decline in lumber prices were believed to be causes of his desperate action. "There is no reason for him to have worried the way he did," business partner Sidney Hauptman reflected. "The cut in rates came at a time when he was in ill health and caused him to take a much worse view of things than was necessary."

Hauptman turned his company's little fleet of ships over to Charles R. McCormick. McCormick was a childhood friend of Hauptman and his brother George in Saginaw, Michigan. According to one biographer, "They were part of a group of lumbermen from the Midwest who left the dwindling white pine forests of their home states for the virgin Douglas Fir stands of the Pacific."

McCormick migrated to Portland, Oregon in 1901. A few months later, he traveled to San Francisco to accept a position with the Hammond Lumber Company. Eager to branch out on his own, he left Hammond in 1903 to establish a lumber brokerage firm with Sidney Hauptman called Charles R. McCormick & Company. He also helped organize the McCormick-Hauptman Lumber Company with his childhood friends. When Sidney partnered later with Earl Hicks, George remained with the enterprise as the other half of McCormick-Hauptman.

Challenging Business

In July 1916, the newly formed steamship brokerage firm of Fair & Moran acquired control of a small fleet of schooners which included the *J.B. Stetson*. "Wholesale lumber steamship agents," one of their ads read. "Orders for coastwise and foreign shipments solicited."

Fair & Moran sold their fleet in early 1918 to the Gulf Mail Steamship Company. The venture kept the *J.B. Stetson* busily plying the waters between San Francisco, Central America, and the Panama Canal. She also carried cargo to Peruvian ports, "having aboard 350,000 feet of redwood for Callao and 9,000 ties for Lima."

The *J.B. Stetson* was purchased by the A.B. Johnson Company in March 1923. Abraham Bertram Johnson entered the lumber and shipping business in Portland, Oregon as a partner in Wilson Brothers & Company. The family enterprise began in the 1860s after five siblings immigrated to the United States from Sweden, changed their last name from Olsson to Wilson, and created ventures which spread into Aberdeen, Washington, Portland, Oregon, and San Francisco, California.

Fred Wilson, the first sibling to depart Swedish shores, sailed from England to America in 1861. In Oregon, he gained work aboard a wharf boat handling freight. "It was very hard work," Fred acknowledged. "A cook on an old steamer took pity on me and made me a cook on the boat. The cook soon left and he recommended me to the captain for the place of deck hand."

After that, Fred found steady employment, rising to the position of ship's master for the Oregon Steam Navigation Company. By 1869, he had sufficient savings to return to Sweden to bring his brother John and sister Bertha to America. He also called for his seafaring brothers Charles and Henry to join him in a tow boat business in Portland. In addition to this endeavor, the group established a sawmill and lumberyard, and the family company, Wilson Brothers, was born.

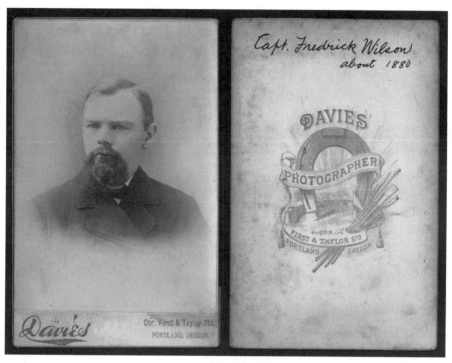

Fred Wilson and four siblings established a family lumber company called Wilson Brothers. Their operations extended through Washington, Oregon and California. Wilson Brothers Family Foundation.

The clan expanded operations in the 1880s at Gray's Harbor on the southwest coast of Washington. They opened a lumber business in Aberdeen under Charles' direction while the lumberyard in Portland continued under Henry's management. A.B. Johnson, the brother of Henry's new wife, joined the family team and the firm became Wilson Brothers & Company.

As the Aberdeen facility continued to grow, Henry Wilson and Johnson moved the lumberyard from Portland to San Francisco. "The duo endured trials and tribulations while expanding and managing their successful lumber and shipping venture from two sites separated by more than six hundred miles," Emily Wilson, a descendant of Charles Wilson revealed. "The structure of their business was challenged by a volatile lumber market, legal battles, employee unrest, competitive business practices, and the illness and death of Charles Wilson."

In the early 1900s, Wilson Brothers & Company split into separate California and Washington enterprises. In California, Henry Wilson turned his portion of the business over to his two sons. Johnson left the firm to build his own lumber networks and operate schooners in the coastwise lumber trade.

Merciless Foe

On more than one occasion, Johnson nearly lost the *J.B. Stetson*. In November 1927, the vessel limped into San Francisco, bringing a tale of a terrific battle with a severe storm off the Oregon coast. Capt. Carl Hubner said his crew of twenty men fought for their lives in a seventy mile gale off Astoria. With a wrecked deckhouse and shattered masts, the waterlogged schooner barely made port under her own power. All continued to go well for another few years.

Then, on May 29, 1933 the *J.B. Stetson* collided with the steamship *Chehalis* off the fog-bound coast of Santa Barbara, California. The master of the *Chehalis* beached the vessel to prevent her from sinking. "She was aground broadside to the beach and appeared to be a total loss," news reports stated. "The lumber schooner *J. B. Stetson* steamed into the outer harbor, apparently undamaged, and headed for her Long Beach harbor dock."

Just over a year later, on September 3, 1934, the *J.B. Stetson* faced her final fight with the sea. The schooner was creeping through a dense fog blanketing the mid-California coast, when she was caught in the grip of an onshore current and rammed into the jagged rocks of Point

A.B. Johnson joined the Wilson Brothers' firm before developing his own enterprise. In the early 1900s, he purchased the J.B. Stetson *for use in the coastwise lumber trade.* Wilson Brothers Family Foundation.

The J.B. Stetson *grounded on the wave-lashed beach of Point Pinos in 1934. After a bitter fight with the raging surf, she broke in half and sank.* Gene Barron.

Pinos. The crew felt a sudden shudder and lurch. Those who were off duty below deck were tossed from their bunks by the impact.

Capt. Hubner immediately ordered Chief Engineer Ed Putney to sound a series of distress blasts on the whistle. Under the direction of First Officer Sam Christenson, the crew clambered over the sides on ropes lowered to small lifeboats. Meanwhile, water rushed into the ship through a gaping hole torn in her hull.

Sent to the scene was the U.S. Coast Guard cutter *Daphne* which had been conducting a search for a missing fishing vessel. Launched in 1932, the *Daphne* was part of a class of 165-foot cutters with excellent seagoing qualities and good accommodations for the crew. An article written soon after she entered service boasted, "The new cutters are low, without excessive superstructure. A raking stem, well flared bow, and cruiser stern give the appearance of speed as well as contribute to the seaworthiness of the vessels."

No doubt, she was a welcome sight. The *J.B. Stetson*'s crew rowed to the cutter taking with them the ship's mascot, a dog named Flossie. Since ancient times, dogs, as well as cats, have been mascots on many trading, fishing, exploration, and naval vessels. They were an important part of the crew because they helped control rodents which could damage ropes and woodwork, devour foodstuffs, and carry disease. Dogs and cats also offered valuable companionship and a sense of home, security and camaraderie to sailors who could be away from home for long periods.

Satisfied that Flossie and the crew were rescued, Capt. Hubner remained aboard the stricken craft. Three hours later, when it became clear the schooner was sinking, the skipper abandoned ship at the behest of the *Daphne*'s commanding officer. Three days later, a heavy sea finally broke the back of the *J.B. Stetson*, sending two automobiles and $5,000 in general merchandise tumbling into the water. After a bitter fight with the raging surf, the ship succumbed, breaking in two amidships.

"The steam schooner *J.B. Stetson* crashed upon the ragged reefs about a hundred yards from where the lumber schooner *Flavel* met a similar fate in 1924," a local newspaper observed. "The *Stetson* was a familiar figure in local ports for nearly three decades. Fog, grim, grey merciless foe of all navigators, claimed another victim."

Capt. Carl Hubner abandoned the stricken J.B. Stetson *only after he was satisfied that the crew and the ship's mascot, a dog named Flossie, were rescued.* Gene Barron.

12

OTHER SHIPWRECKS

Between 1907 and 1944, nine additional shipwrecks, craft sinkings, and near-misses occurred near Point Pinos. Although there is little information about them, the incidents are worth noting. The ships include the steamer *Bonita*, the fishing vessels *Ida May, Italia* and *New Crivello*, the schooners *Tamalpais* and *Aurora*, the Navy patrol boat *YP-128*, and two unidentified Army amphibious craft.

BONITA — November 12, 1907

"The steamer *Bonita*, while placing a buoy for an oil company, got on the rocks near the oil wharf, but got off uninjured," Keeper Emily Fish reported on November 12, 1907. "Weather cloudy, heavy seas, and haze."

Through some miscalculation, the *Bonita* drifted too close to the pinnacles of Point Pinos. Jagged rocks broke a hole through her hull. For more than three hours, the steamer hung on while the crew worked desperately at the pumps to keep her from sinking. Capt. Carey feared that the ship would soon fill with water completely. Fortunately, the tug *Dauntless* arrived in time to tow the *Bonita* into port. Further examination showed her damage to be slight.

Later, Capt. Carey mentioned another hair-raising incident from the previous day. The skipper discovered he was sailing squarely between members of a coast defense battery and its target, a wrecked pile driver. "I threw myself at the whistle cord and used up a lot of steam telling them to look out for the *Bonita*," the captain explained. "We were out of range in a few minutes, but my hair has been standing up ever since."

IDA MAY — August 29, 1930

Many shipbuilders found the waters of Washington's Puget Sound an ideal location. Among them, were F.M. Crawford and James Reid who established themselves as ship carpenters, caulkers, and spar makers in Tacoma. By 1908, they were building fishing schooners such as the *Ida May*. Intended for the halibut fishing trade, the schooner measured 62 tons, was 73 feet long, 18 feet wide, and carried a crew of eleven. According to one account, "She was equipped with a seventy-six horsepower engine and fitted with electric lights and other conveniences not common to vessels of the fishing fleet."

The *Ida May* was fashioned for the Pacific Net & Twine Company of Seattle, which had become an important supplier of marine and fishing gear. The enterprise was founded in 1897 by Edward Cunningham, a twenty-one year-old Scottish immigrant, and D.B. McBride of Portland, Oregon. Run out of a basement, the business was originally limited to selling netting and twine. The duo moved their growing operation to Seattle's waterfront in 1904 to begin supplying the Puget Sound and Alaskan fishing industries.

As fate would have it, the *Ida May*'s first voyage was quite dramatic. On September 30, 1908, she collided in dense fog with the Canadian Pacific steamer *Princess Victoria* roughly fifteen miles north of Seattle. The schooner was returning from her maiden voyage to the halibut banks of the Bering Strait with 30,000 pounds of fish.

Cut nearly in half, the *Ida May* settled in the water slowly. The frightened fishermen clambered pell-mell up the anchor chains and ropes of the *Princess Victoria*. Without hesitation, Capt. Griffin dispatched some of his crew over the side to bring the fishermen aboard. Others shimmied onto the deck of the *Ida May*, lashing the schooner to the steamer to prevent her from sinking. As the steamer pushed the fishing vessel toward shore, a crowd of spectators filled the deck. The rescued fishermen stood among them.

Built by Crawford & Reid in 1908, the Ida May *was a halibut fishing schooner. She went aground at Point Pinos in 1930.* Puget Sound Maritime Historical Society.

For several years, the *Ida May* continued in the halibut fishing trade. In 1911, she was purchased by the Columbia & Northern Fishing & Packing Company of Rainier, Oregon. The schooner's new owner, F. Klevenhusen, served as president of the firm and held extensive fishing interests throughout Oregon. He re-powered the *Ida May* for deep-sea fishing, strategically basing her near the mouth of the Columbia River at Astoria.

In 1917, Klevenhusen found new commercial opportunities in California. He established a cold storage plant for salmon along the Noyo River near Fort Bragg in Mendocino County. Representing an investment of $12,000, the plant had a cold storage capacity of 125 tons. The *Ida May* became a frequent visitor at small ports along the California coast.

On August 29, 1930, the *Ida May* ran into unidentified difficulties near Point Pinos. The incident eluded newspapers entirely. All that is known is that she "stranded with one person onboard at Pacific Grove with no loss of life."

TAMALPAIS — March 21, 1931

The schooner *Tamalpais* was constructed in 1906 by Matthews Shipbuilding Company of Hoquiam, Washington. Hoquiam, a Native-American word meaning "hungry for wood," is located near Gray's Harbor and borders the city of Aberdeen. Appropriately, the town's economic history is based in lumbering and shipping.

About 1897, Peter Matthews created a shipyard in Hoquiam to build lumber carriers for the E.K. Wood Lumber Company. Edwin K. Wood's firm established docks in Oakland and San Pedro, operated yards and mills in Los Angeles, Oakland, San Rafael, Fresno, San Francisco, and Bellingham, Washington, and owned a fleet of vessels that hauled cargo up and down the coast.

For years, the *Tamalpais* made countless runs from Gray's Harbor to San Pedro, California via San Francisco carrying lumber and general freight. Although most trips were relatively uneventful, they were not without occasional difficulty. On November 26, 1920, the fully loaded schooner was departing San Pedro when she was blown ashore by gusty winds. After the captain reported the vessel as waterlogged, a tug was sent to tow her to up the coast to Hoquiam where cargo was discharged and repairs were made.

The schooner Tamalpais *stranded on a sandbar at Moss Landing in 1932. Fifty-thousand feet of lumber was thrown overboard to save her from sinking.* Pacific Grove Museum of Natural History.

From 1923 to 1931, the *Tamalpais* served the Little River Redwood Company of Humboldt County, California. Later, the enterprise became the Hammond-Little River Redwood Company, Ltd. in a merger with the Hammond Lumber Company. Established by timber baron Andrew B. Hammond, the firm was one of the largest lumber companies on the West Coast.

On March 21, 1931, Capt. Adolf Ahlin was attempting to steer the *Tamalpais* from the Moss Landing pier when he noticed her broken rudder. Waves swept the 574-ton schooner fifty yards onto a sandbank. To lighten the ship's load, fifty-thousand feet of lumber was thrown overboard. According to a local newspaper, "The captain and crew of eighteen remained aboard throughout the night."

The following day, the tug *Ranger* succeeded in pulling the stranded vessel off the sandbar and towing her to San Francisco. Once there, she was broken up for scrap.

ITALIA — February 28, 1933

As dawn broke on February 28, 1933, two fishermen set out from Monterey bound for Carmel Bay. Aboard their 27-foot fishing boat *Italia*, they lost their bearings in the fog, drifted in too close to the treacherous currents off Point Pinos, and foundered on a reef where the surf breaks in five directions at once.

Wreckage was strewn for half a mile along the shore. The bodies of Nino Bellici and Nino Carnello were pulled from the breakers by rescuers who braved the snarling undertow. Although both men had fished on sardine crews for years, the fatal voyage was only their second down the coast.

AURORA — January 18, 1935

A four-masted barkentine, the 1,211 ton *Aurora* was fashioned at Everett, Washington in 1901. She was commissioned by the Charles Nelson Company of San Francisco, a large lumber shipping business that once owned the *William H. Smith*. Converted to a schooner around 1920, the *Aurora* was owned by Nelson during her entire sea life.

In 1927, she was laid up at San Francisco and sold five years later to become a tourist attraction. On January 18, 1935, the *Aurora* broke her moorings in Monterey Bay and smashed ashore during a gale. The ship's loss was not only an historic one, but an aesthetic one.

The Aurora *was built as a four-masted barkentine in 1901 for Charles Nelson's large lumber shipping company.* Gene Barron.

The Aurora *was converted to a schooner and later sold to become a tourist attraction. During a gale in 1935, she ran aground in Monterey Bay.* Pacific Grove Museum of Natural History.

Along with the *William H. Smith*, the *Aurora* was one of two tall-masted ships whose presence in the harbor added a picturesque touch to the waterfront. One writer lamented, "The *Aurora* was reduced to a rather dubious amusement ship. Once, she was a sailing ship with her canvas full against the sky."

NEW CRIVELLO — September 18, 1936

Carrying fifty tons of sardines, the *New Crivello* went ashore in Monterey on September 18, 1936. Owned by Joe G. Crivello, the fishing vessel was launched only a few weeks before the mishap. Thousands of dead sardines lined the beach after the wreck. "The sea gulls were quick to discover this free feed," one newspaper commented, "and came in brigades to take advantage of it."

Capt. Mike Lucido blamed heavy fog for the accident. Others thought the fog signal at Point Pinos was at fault, claiming that a siren type signal was difficult to hear. For years, fishing captains had wanted a fog signal which could be heard at sea. "After the *New Crivello* wrecked within a quarter mile of the fog signal, the matter was again brought forcefully to local attention," the *Monterey Peninsula Herald* asserted. "When a new air horn was installed in 1939, there could be no happier news to Monterey fishermen."

Luckily, Capt. Lucido and ten crew made their way to shore in a skiff. Refloated three days later by the tug *Sea Salvor*, the ship seemed saved, as well. Partially submerged, the 116-ton vessel was towed toward San Francisco for repairs. Unfortunately, the *Sea Salvor*'s slings snapped while passing Pigeon Point Lighthouse. On September 24, 1936, the *New Crivello* sank two miles north of the tower.

YP-128 — June 30, 1942

During World War II, the beacons of lighthouses across America were extinguished to protect the country's borders from possible attack. Since lighthouses were placed strategically along the nation's shoreline, the U.S. Coast Guard established beach patrols and lookout stations at many of the sites.

One of them was Point Pinos where a coastal artillery battery and Coast Guard Beach Patrol unit operated. Complete with barracks, horse stables, and dog kennels, the lookout station was manned twenty-four hours a day, seven days a week. The north upstairs bedroom of the

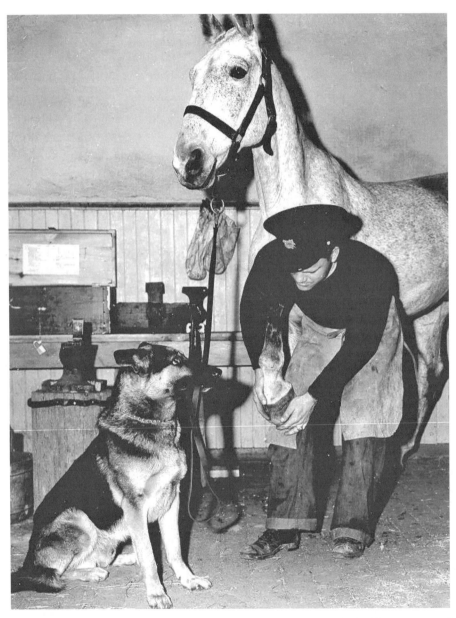

During World War II, an artillery battery and Coast Guard Beach Patrol unit operated at Point Pinos complete with barracks, horse stables, and dog kennels. United States Coast Guard.

lighthouse served as the command post. Among the unusual events that occurred were the sinking of the *YP-128* in 1942 and two amphibious craft in 1944.

A U.S. Navy patrol boat, the *YP-128* was built in 1935 as the *Bonnie Dundee III*. The 44-ton vessel was constructed by the well-known firm of Luders Marine Construction. Alfred E. Luders began his shipyard in 1908 with twenty-five employees and a thousand dollars of capital. The yard established a broad reputation for its fine custom built yachts.

During World War I, the Luders yard won a naval patrol craft design contest sponsored by Franklin D. Roosevelt, then Assistant Secretary of the Navy. The company also built barges for seaplanes that were to be towed behind destroyers. In 1924, the company built ten 75-foot patrol boats for the Coast Guard that were used to pursue rum runners and smugglers. In World War II the yard had as many as 1,200 employees and turned out more than eighty vessels. These included subchasers, minesweepers, patrol craft, harbor tugs and tow-target boats.

Charles Day Mallory, Sr. owned the *Bonnie Dundee*. He was part of a long family line with interests in shipping and shipbuilding which centered its activities in Mystic, Connecticut and New York. Mallory was active in a variety of executive positions with the Clyde and the Mallory Steamship Lines, served as assistant director of operations of the United States Shipping Board Emergency Fleet Corporation, and was President of C.D. Mallory & Company. Along with his shipping interests, he had a great interest in yachting and was also a noted philanthropist.

After Mallory passed away in 1941, the *Bonnie Dundee* was acquired by the Navy for war time use and re-named the *YP-128*. The designation YP meant a yard patrol craft. Initially, the vessels were used for inshore and harbor patrol activities. During World War II, the fleet grew to about 650, mostly by the acquisition and conversion of private fishing vessels and yachts.

The *YP-128* became the flag ship for the Surface Task Group, Northern Sector, Western Sea Frontier Patrol Force. The patrol group was headquartered at the Treasure Island Naval Base near San Francisco. According to now declassified documents, "The purpose of the patrol is to observe and report enemy air activity and to rescue personnel of our own aircraft in distress."

On June 30, 1942, the *YP-128* became lost in fog and ran aground three miles northeast of Monterey. Apparently, the patrol boat was attempting to recover a Coast Guard whistle buoy, "Point Pinos #2," reported to be adrift. Whistle buoys were first adopted by the Lighthouse

Board in 1877. The buoy's whistle was activated by the action of the sea, enabling a mariner to determine a ship's position. If for some reason, the buoy drifted, vessels could be lured off course and even into disaster.

Laying broadside to the beach, the battered patrol boat's engine room and crew quarters filled rapidly with water. After five attempts to refloat her proved ineffective, the ship's equipment was salvaged. Slowly, the *YP-128* slipped under the sea and was stricken from the Navy list of vessels.

Amphibious Craft — June 7, 1944

In 1917, the U.S. Army purchased land just north of Monterey for use as an artillery training field. The site was known as the U.S. Field Artillery Area, Presidio of Monterey and Gigling Field Artillery Range. In 1933, the field became Camp Ord, named for Maj. Gen. Edward Ord, a Union Army leader during the Civil War. Horse cavalry units trained on the camp until the military began to mechanize and train mobile combat units.

In 1940, Camp Ord was expanded and renamed Fort Ord. The 7th Infantry Division was reactivated, becoming the first major unit to occupy the post. For the next thirty years, the fort served as a primary West Coast facility for training Army troops. During World War II, "Amtrac" and "Amtank" battalions were trained in rigorous amphibious assault operations. Monterey Bay was often "stormed" during field maneuvers.

Amtracs and Amtanks were a class of small amphibious tractors and tanks used as landing craft for ship to shore operations. Originally intended solely as cargo carriers, they rapidly evolved into assault troop and fire support vehicles as well. Historian Harry Yiede observed, "Equipped with tanks, amphibian tanks, and amphibian tractors, these units went everywhere the Army went, from the beginning of the war to its very end."

On June 7, 1944, two of the craft were lost about six hundred yards off Point Pinos during Fort Ord training maneuvers. According to now declassified documents, "A blimp from Moffett Field, on routine patrol, was diverted to conduct a brief search for two amphibious craft sunk off Point Pinos. The search, made at the request of the Army, was fruitless."

The blimp was Airship *K-47*, part of a class of non-rigid airships built by the Goodyear Aircraft Company of Akron, Ohio for the U.S.

Monterey's Fort Ord was named for Maj. Gen. Edward Ord, a Civil War hero. The fort was a U.S. Army training facility for early artillery and cavalry units. During World War II, it became a training center for amphibious assault Operations. Library of Congress.

Navy. Non-rigid airships were flexible and held in shape only by internal gas pressure. Before and during World War II, 135 K-class blimps were configured for patrol and anti-submarine warfare operations and were used extensively in both the Atlantic and Pacific Oceans.

Interestingly, the *K-47*'s control car cockpit was restored after being pulled from a scrap yard near a naval air station at Lakehurst, New Jersey. The cockpit is on display at the National Aviation Museum in Pensacola, Florida. "*K-47* is part of the most widely produced class of airships in naval aviation history," museum officials explained. "As the backbone of the Navy's lighter than air operations during World War II, K-ships flew antisubmarine patrols over convoys and logged many an air-sea rescue flight."

AUTHOR'S NOTE

The shipwrecks and waters surrounding Point Pinos are protected by the Monterey Bay National Marine Sanctuary. Spanning more than 5,300 square miles, the Sanctuary provides a safe haven for the area's marine life, coastal environments, and cultural history.

As part of its Maritime Heritage Program, the Sanctuary has developed a database of 463 reported vessel losses that lie within its jurisdiction, or adjacent to its boundaries. "Upon wrecking, vessels are known to drift at least fifteen miles," the database emphasizes. "Therefore, losses located just to the north of the Sanctuary in Marin County and just to the south of the Sanctuary in San Luis Obispo County are included."

Describing hundreds of maritime mishaps is beyond the scope of this book. The shipwrecks discussed here were selected based on available records, reports of lighthouse keepers, and relevance to Point Pinos.

EPILOGUE

Point Pinos Lighthouse is located in Pacific Grove, a coastal town at the tip of the Monterey Peninsula. The area was described in 1847 by young Army Lt. William T. Sherman, a future Civil War hero, as "shaped like a fishhook." Viewed from south to north, Pacific Grove dangles from the barb and Monterey snuggles the curve. Fort Ord and Seaside hug the shore where the hook bends away from the peninsula, and Santa Cruz anchors the shank.

By the mid-1800s, Monterey had become a bustling port, while Pacific Grove remained relatively quiet and unpopulated well after the lighthouse was built in 1855. A road, which became known as Lighthouse Avenue, was constructed in 1874 to reach the tower. The city was established in 1875 and incorporated in 1889.

Often referred to as one of America's "last hometowns," Pacific Grove is known for its Victorian homes, beautiful beaches, artistic legacy, and annual migration of the Monarch butterflies. The city lists over 1,200 historic structures on its official Historic Register as well as a half-dozen structures on the National Historic Register, including Point Pinos Lighthouse.

Point Pinos opened as a museum in 1983. Since then, dedicated lighthouse docents, volunteers from the Adobe Chapter of the California

Questers, and members of the Pacific Grove Heritage Society have spent countless hours restoring the tower, lantern room, keeper's quarters, oil house, and surrounding grounds and garden. Local families donated historic artifacts and valuable antiques while businesses contributed labor and materials.

The beacon's preservation has become an important community endeavor. According to the Heritage Society, "The City of Pacific Grove has been given this historic building in its spectacular setting. In time, we hope to bring this treasure back to its former glory days."

Today, Point Pinos stands as a significant symbol of California's early history and diverse maritime commerce. Each flash of its bright light gives us pause to reflect on the special people and unique events that are part of our local lore and deep coastal roots.

Point Pinos Lighthouse is an historic treasure. Each flash of its beacon reflects the people and the events that are part of our local lore and deep coastal roots. Photo taken from the watch room, facing the ocean. Author's Collection.

Photo courtesy of Julie Barrow.

ABOUT THE AUTHOR

JoAnn Semones, Ph.D., boarded her first ship at age three. The voyage, made aboard the *E.D. Patrick*, left a lasting impression. She has loved sea sagas ever since. Her other books, *Sea of Troubles, Shipwrecks, Scalawags, and Scavengers*, and *Hard Luck Coast*, focus on shipwrecks at the Point Sur, Pigeon Point, and Point Montara lighthouses.

As a consultant with the Monterey Bay National Marine Sanctuary and California State Parks, she has written interpretive materials for exhibits at Pigeon Point Light Station State Historic Park and Año Nuevo State Park. She is featured in a video highlighting local maritime history which is part of a new permanent exhibit entitled "Ships of the World" at the San Mateo County History Museum.

JoAnn's stories have appeared in a variety of publications, including *Mains'L Haul, Professional Mariner, Lighthouse Digest, Anchor Light, La Peninsula, Journal of Local History, Good Old Days Magazine, A Light In The Mist*, and *Surviving Magazine*, as well as in Stanford University's anthology, *Learning to Live Again*, and in the *Chicken Soup for the Soul* international book series.

Visit her website at: *www.GullCottageBooks.com.*

Appendix

Those Who Were Lost

Natalia – December 21, 1834

Unidentified – cook
Unidentified – two sailors

Julius Pringle – September 27, 1863

Unidentified – one sailor

Italia – March 2, 1933

Nino Bellici – fisherman
Nino Carnello – fisherman

BIBLIOGRAPHY

General

"Aids to Navigation," WPA Historical Survey of the Monterey Peninsula, July 26, 1937.

Ball, Edmund F. *California Gold Rush Diary of Charles H. Harvey*. Indianapolis, Indiana: Indiana Historical Society. 1983.

Bancroft, Hubert Howe. *History of California 1825-1840*. San Francisco: History Company, 1884.

Black, Frederick Frasier. *Searsport Sea Captains*. Searsport, Maine: Penobscot Marine Museum, 1960.

Clark, Donald T. *Monterey County Place Names*. Carmel Valley, California: Kestrel Press, 1991.

Clifford, Mary Louise and J. Candace. *Women Who Kept the Lights*. Williamsburg, Virginia: Cypress Communications, 1993.

"Death of Mrs. Charlotte A. Harris," *Monterey Cypress*, February 15, 1896.

"Emily Fish: Keeper of Point Pinos Lighthouse," *Monterey Peninsula Herald*, September 3, 1978.

Gibbs, James A. *Shipwrecks of the Pacific Coast*. Portland, Oregon: Binfords & Mort, 1962.

"George C. Harris, a Pioneer of '46," *Monterey Cypress*, December 17, 1890.

"Hill-Bound Monterey," *San Francisco Chronicle*, April 4, 1875.

"Historic Light," *Monterey Peninsula Herald*, December 16, 1964.

Holland, Francis Ross. *America's Lighthouses*. New York, New York: Dover Publications, 1988.

Lewis, Oscar. *Sea Routes to the Gold Fields*. New York, New York, Alfred A. Knopf, 1949.

Lloyd's Register of American and Foreign Shipping. London, England: Wyman & Sons, various years.

Lubbock, Basil. *Last of the Windjammers*. Glasgow, Scotland: Brown, Son & Ferguson, 1953.

Lyman, John. Pacific Coast Steam Schooners, 1884-1924. Seattle, Washington: *Marine Digest*, 1943.

Marshall, Don B. *California Shipwrecks*. Seattle, Washington: Superior Publishing Company, 1978.

Martin, Wallace E. *Sail and Steam on the Northern California Coast, 1850-1900*. San Francisco, California: National Maritime Association, 1983.

Matthews, Frederick C., *American Merchant Ships*, Volumes I and II. Salem, Massachusetts: Marine Research Society, 1930.

McCaffery, Jerry. *Point Pinos Lighthouse*. Pacific Grove, California: Hana Media Group, 2001.

McNairn, Jack and MacMullen, Jerry. *Ships of the Redwood Coast*. Stanford, California: Stanford University Press, 1970.

Newell, Gordon. *The H.W. McCurdy Marine History of the Pacific Northwest*. Seattle, Washington: Superior Publishing Company, 1986.

"On Point Pinos," WPA Historical Survey of Point Pinos, April 27, 1937.

"Point Pinos Lighthouse," *This Month on the Monterey Peninsula*, August 1983.

"Point Pinos Lighthouse Celebrates 100th Anniversary," paper prepared by Monterey Public Library, August 1954.

"Point Pinos Light Station," *Monterey Peninsula Herald*, January 19, 1992.

"Point Pinos – West's Oldest Lighthouse," *Herald Weekend Magazine*, August 28, 1977.

Reinstedt, Randall. *Shipwrecks and Sea Monsters*. Carmel, California: Ghost Town Publications, 1975.

Rowe, William Hutchinson. *The Maritime History of Maine*. New York, New York: W.W. Norton & Company, 1948.

"Sentinels of the Central Coast," *Monterey Life*, September 1980.

Shipwreck Data Base, National Marine Sanctuary Program, National Oceanic and Atmospheric Administration.

Stevenson, Robert Louis. *Across the Plains with Other Memories and Essays*. London, England: Chatto and Windus, 1892.

Stumbo, Jean Serpell. *Emily Fish, Socialite Lighthouse Keeper*. Pacific Grove, California: Pacific Grove Museum of Natural History Association, 1997.

"Welcome to Point Pinos Lighthouse," *Monterey Peninsula Review*, December 8, 1983.

"Women's Work: Female Lighthouse Keepers in the Early Republic," Master of Arts Thesis by Virginia Neal Thomas, Old Dominion University, December 2010.

Wright, E.W. *Lewis and Dryden's Marine History of the Pacific Northwest*. New York, New York: Antiquarian Press, 1961.

Natalia – June 21, 1834

"A Piece of Polished Wood from Napoleon's *Natalia*," *Monterey Peninsula Herald*, April 30, 1951.

"Asleep in the Deep," *Monterey Peninsula Herald*," April 23, 1951.

Beebe, Rose Marie and Senkewicz, Robert M. *Testimonios: Early California Through the Eyes of Women, 1815-1848*. Berkeley, California: Heyday Books, 2006.

Bouvier, Virginia M. *Women and the Conquest of California:1542-1840*. Tucson, Arizona: University of Arizona Press, 2001.

"California Colonization Laws," document from the Primera Secretaria de Estado, Departamento del Interior, October 26, 1833.

Hutchinson, C. Alan. *Manifesto to the Mexican Republic*. Berkeley, California: University of California Press, 1978.

"Most Famous Vessel Ever Wrecked on the Pacific Coast," *San Francisco Chronicle*, August 2, 1914.

"Napoleon's Ship *Natalia*," *Monterey Peninsula Herald*, April 16, 1969.

"*Natalia*," State of California Shipwreck Website, May 30, 2006.

"*Natalia* Legend Sunk," *Monterey Peninsula Herald*, September 16, 1971.

"*Natalia*'s Grave in Monterey Bay," *Monterey Peninsula Herald*, October 25, 1963.

"Pioneer Spanish Families of California," *Journal of San Diego History*, June 1965.

"Ships That Made California History 1607-1848," manuscript compiled from H.H. Bancroft's works by Work Progress Administration, Monterey, California, 1937.

"Wreck of the Good Ship *Natalia*," *Monterey Peninsula Herald*, October 23, 1963.

Commodore Rogers – October 18, 1837

"Brig *Commodore Rogers* Driven on Shore," *Monterey Weekly Herald*, January 1, 1875.

"*Commodore Rogers*," State of California Shipwreck Website, 2010.

"Ships That Made California History 1607-1848," manuscript compiled from H.H. Bancroft's works by Work Progress Administration, Monterey, California, 1937.

Starbuck, Alexander. *History of American Whale Fishery*. New York, New York: Argosy-Antiquarian, 1964.

Star of the West – July 27, 1845

American Trust Company. *American Trust Review of the Pacific*, Volumes 10-11. San Francisco, California: Savings Union Bank and Trust Company, 1921.

"A Small Fortune from a Total Wreck," *Monterey Peninsula Herald*, July 24, 1951.

Clarke, S.J. *History of San Mateo County*. Chicago, Illinois, S.J. Clarke Publishing Co., 1928.

"Ships That Made California History 1607-1848," manuscript compiled from H.H. Bancroft's works by Work Progress Administration, Monterey, California, 1937.

"Smuggling was Big Business," *Monterey Peninsula Herald*, June 1, 1970.

Rochelle – December 1, 1849

"California Bound," *New York Herald*, February 6, 1849.

"Commodore John Paty: Merchant Mariner," *Hawaiian Journal of History*, 2006.

Donnelley, R.R. *Seventy-Five Years in California*. Chicago, Illinois: Lakeside Press, 1928.

Davis, William Heath. *Sixty Years in California*. San Francisco, California: A.J. Leary, 1889.

"Emigration to El Dorado," *New York Herald*, April 19, 1849.

"Marine Disasters," *Alta California*, December 1, 1849.

"There is a Seafaring Man," *Trestleboard*, June 2008.

"Trade Without Law," *Journal of Law, Economics, and Organization*, 1997.

Julius Pringle – September 27, 1863

Bagley, Clarence. *History of Seattle*. Seattle, Washington: S.J. Clarke Publishing Company, 1916.

"Breakers Ahead: A Decade of Marine Disaster," *Sunday Chronicle*, September 30, 1877.

Coman, Edwin T. and Gibbs, Helen M. *Time, Tide, and Timber*. Stanford, California: Stanford University Press, 1949.

Cutler, Carl C. *Queens of the Western Ocean*. Annapolis, Maryland: Naval Institute Press, 1961.

Hurd, D. Hamilton. *History of New London County, Connecticut*. Philadelphia, Pennsylvania: J.B. Lippincott & Company, 1882.

"Port Gamble, Washington." *Washington History Quarterly*, January 1925.

"Schooner *Julius Pringle* Ashore," *Daily Alta California*, September 30, 1863.

Silver Cloud – September 24, 1878

"Along the Wharves," *Daily Alta California*, September 25, 1878.

"List of Vessels Injured and Lost During 1878," *Alta California*, January 2, 1879.

"Schooner Ashore," *Daily Alta California*, September 25, 1878.

U.S. Coast Guard. *Merchant Vessels of the United States*. Washington, D.C., Government Printing Office: July 1872 to December 1873.

Ivanhoe – **September 20, 1891**

"Afloat & Ashore," *San Francisco Call*, October 30, 1900.

Bancroft, Hubert H. *History of Oregon*. San Francisco, California: History Company, 1888.

"Death of Charles M. Pershbaker," *The Oregonian*, October 7, 1870.

Gaston, Joseph. *The Centennial History of Oregon*. Chicago, Illinois: S.J. Clark Publishing, 1912.

Jackson, Walter A. *Doghole Schooners*. Volcano, California: California Traveler, 1969.

Lorentzen, A.P. Deposition before fur seal arbitration, October 18, 1892.

"Lumbering," *Oregon History Project*, 2006.

MacGillivray, Don. *Captain Alex MacLean: Jack London's Sea Wolf*. Vancouver, British Columbia: University of British Columbia, 2008.

"Oregon's Shipbuilding," *The Oregonian*, February 19, 1901.

"Report Received," *Morning Call*, January 5, 1893.

"Schooner *Ivanhoe* Ashore," *Morning Call*, September 22, 1891.

"Schooners *Sea Foam* and *Humboldt*," *Mendocino Beacon*, 3 October 1885.

"Schooner Wrecked," *Sacramento Daily Union*, January 5, 1893.

"The Sea Wolf," *Tales from the Vault*, Greater Victoria Library, May 2011.

"Towed to Monterey," *San Francisco Call*, September 22, 1891.

Walling, A.G. *History of Southern Oregon*. Hong Kong, China: Forgotten Books, 2013.

Alexander Duncan – **November 6, 1892**

"All Stormbound," *San Francisco Morning Call*, November 30, 1892.

Best, Gerald M. *Ships and Narrow Gauge Rails*. Berkeley, California: Howell-North, 1964.

"Captain Nicolson's Statement," *Daily Alta California*, September 17, 1885.

"Captains in the Port of San Francisco," *The Maritime Heritage Project*, 1998.

Dodds, Gordon B. *The Salmon King of Oregon*. Chapel Hill, North Carolina: University of North Carolina Press, 1959.

"Marine News," *Los Angeles Herald*, November 13,1883.

"Steamer *Alexander Duncan*," *Morning Call*, September 21, 1885.

"Steamer *Alexander Duncan*," *Sacramento Daily Union*, September 10, 1885.

"Steamer *Alexander Duncan* Goes Ashore," *Daily Alta California*, September 9, 1885.

"Steamer *Alexander Duncan* Saved," *Morning Call*, September 20, 1885.

"Struck a Snag," *San Francisco Call*, May 26, 1891.

"Suspended for a Shipwreck," *Daily Alta California*, October 29, 1885.

"Wreck of the *Duncan*," *Daily Alta California*, September 15, 1885.

"Wrecked *Alexander Duncan*," *Morning Call*, September 11, 1885.

St. Paul – August 8, 1896

"Captain Downing Loses His Papers," *Monterey Cypress*, August 29, 1896.

"Cramp Shipyard, a Community Organization and a Community Institution," Historical Society of Pennsylvania, 2010.

"Lew Kew Sails for Homeland," *Pacific Grove Tribune*, March 25, 1932.

"Old Lighthouse Keeper Passes," *Pacific Grove Tribune*, June 24, 1931.

"Scotsman Revisits Peninsula Scene Where He was Shipwrecked in 1889," *Monterey Peninsula Herald*, circa 1956.

"Shipwreck," *What's Doing*, February 1947.

"Steamer *St. Paul* Wrecked Near Point Pinos," *Monterey Cypress*, August 15, 1896.

"Steamship *St. Paul*," *Pacific Grove/Pebble Beach Tribune*, August 3, 1983.

Northland – September 18, 1904

Atlas Steamship Company. New York, New York: Giles Litho and Liberty Printing Company, 1882.

Bay of San Francisco. Chicago, Illinois: Lewis Publishing Company, 1892.

Carey, Charles H. *History of Oregon*. Chicago, Illinois: Pioneer Historical Publishing Company, 1922.

"Conflict of Stories in *Northland* Case," *San Francisco Call*, September 29, 1904.

"Damage to *Northland*," *Coast Seaman's Journal*, October 12, 1904.

"E.J. Dodge," *Eel Valley Advance*, May 30, 1896.

"Eel River Valley Lumber Company," *Eel River Advance*, May 30, 1896.

"Freighter Sinks After Collision," *Modesto Bee*, July 22, 1927.

Gaston, Joseph. *The Centennial History of Oregon*. Chicago, Illinois: Clarke Publishing Company, 1912.

"Inspectors Suspend License," *Coast Seaman's Journal*, October 26, 1904.

"Mate Hedval Loses License," *San Francisco Call*, October 19, 1904.

"Mate Hedval Rubs Out a Ship's Records," *San Francisco Call*, September 28, 1904.

"*Northland* to be Launched," *Humboldt Standard*, June 14, 1904.

"*Northland* Goes Ashore," *San Francisco Call*, September 20, 1904.

"New Steam Schooner *Northland*," *Coast Seaman's Journal*, September 28 ,1904.

"Schooner *Northland* Brought to SF," *Coast Seaman's Journal*, October 5, 1904.

"Shipwreck," *What's Doing*, February 1947.

"Steamer *Northland*," Humboldt Standard, June 16, 1904.

"Waterfront Notes," *San Francisco Call*, September 23, 1904.

"Waterfront Notes," *San Francisco Call*, September 30, 1904.

"Weekly Steamer Service to be Established," *Morning Oregonian*, September 14, 1904.

Wrecked and Water Logged Steamer *Northland* Is Towed," *San Francisco Call*, September 22, 1904.

Gipsy – September 27, 1905

"Aimed *Gipsy* at Sewer," *Herald Tribune*, October 28, 1905.

"Breaking Up Fast," *San Francisco Examiner*, September 29, 1905.

"Central Coast's Narrow-Gauge Lifeline," *Alta Vista Magazine*, May 10, 1992.

"John K. Bulger," *American Marine Engineer*, February 1912.

"Light on Shore Lures Steamer to Her Death," *San Francisco Examiner*, September 30, 1905.

"Local Shipwreck in 1904 Recalled," *Peninsula Daily Herald*, November 5, 1928.

"Old Steamer *Gipsy* Wrecked," *San Francisco Examiner*, September 28, 1905.

"Shipwreck," *What's Doing*, February 1947.

"S.S. *Gipsy*," *The Compass Rose*, Spring 1994.

"Steamer *Gipsy* Has Close Call," *San Francisco Call*, October 30, 1900.

"Steamer Wrecked at New Monterey," *Monterey New Era*, October 4, 1905.

"Steamship *Gipsy* is Lost on Rocky Coast," *Evening News*, September 28, 1905.

"Trial Trip of the Steamer *Gipsy*," *San Francisco Bulletin*, January 5, 1869.

"When the Steamer '*Gypsy*' [*sic*] Docked at New Monterey," *The Grove at High Tide*, October 19, 1928.

Celia – August 28, 1906

"A History of the Beadle Shipping Companies," research by Gene Barron, 1986.

"*Celia* Waterlogged," *Humboldt Standard*, October 25, 1902.

"Disaster," *San Francisco Call*, August 30, 1906.

"Down to the Seas," *Berkeley Historical Society Newsletter*, Spring 2009.

"Little Saved from Wrecked *Celia*," *Monterey New Era*, September 6, 1906.

"Matthew Turner: Benicia's Shipbuilder Extraordinaire," *Historical Articles of Solano County*, March 17, 2002.

"On the Rocks at Moss Beach," *Monterey New Era*, August 30, 1906.

"Shipwreck," *What's Doing*, February 1947.

"Steamer *Celia*," *Mendocino Beacon*, July 20, 1901.

"Steamer *Celia*," *San Francisco Chronicle*, February 27, 1893.

"Steam Schooner *Celia*," *Mendocino Beacon*, February 1, 1906.

"Storm Tossed *Celia* Safe in the Harbor," *Humboldt Standard*, October 28, 1902.

"Success Born of Grief," *Star Beacon*, December 10, 2011.

"Went on South Spit," *Humboldt Standard*, October 17, 1904.

Rhoderick Dhu – April 25, 1909

"After Fifty Years at Sea, Capt. Rock Retires," *San Francisco Call*, September 8, 1898.

"An Ancient Mariner," *Taranaki Herald*, August 14, 1909.

"Arrived from London," *Sydney Morning Herald*, September 8, 1882.

"Becomes a Farmer," *Hawaii Herald*, October 6, 1898.

"Birds of Prey as Ocean Waifs," *The Auk*, April 1, 1901.

"British Ship *Roderick Dhu* Sold to an American Syndicate," *San Francisco Call*, February 13, 1896.

"Eruption at Krakatoa," paper by Royal Society of Great Britain, January 13, 1884.

"Exports – *Rhoderick Dhu*," *Sydney Morning Herald*, January 23, 1882.

"Fate of the Sailing Ship *T.F. Oakes*," *The Oregonian*, November 26, 1933.

"First of Her Kind Afloat," *San Francisco Call*, November 27, 1900.

Gray, Capt. Harry E. Oral interview by the San Francisco Maritime Museum, 1959-1960.

"*Henry B. Hyde*'s Fast Run," *New York Times,* January 1, 1895.

Johnson, Peter. *Memoirs of Captain Peter Johnson*. San Francisco, California: Peter Johnson, 1938.

"Lost at Sea," *Liverpool Daily Post*, January 31, 1896.

McCandless, Michael H. *Well At Least We Tried: The Seaport of Redondo Beach, 1887 to 1912.* Redondo Beach, California: Michael H. McCandless, 2000.

"Oil Barge Grounded on Sand Near Monterey Bay," *Los Angeles Herald*, April 27, 1909.

"*Roderick Dhu* of the Sugar Fleet Makes Good Run from Hilo," *San Francisco Call*, December 21, 1901.

"*Roderick Dhu*'s Voyaging is Over," *San Francisco Call*, April 29, 1909.

"Seas Smash *Roderick Dhu*'s Wheel Injuring Two Seamen," *San Francisco Call*, January 25, 1909.

"Schooner for Redondo Seriously Damaged," *Los Angeles Herald*, January 25, 1909.

"Shipwreck," *What's Doing*, February 1947.

"Steamer Time made by the *Roderick Dhu*," *San Francisco Call*, February 5, 1899.

"Story of Hawaii and its Builders," *Honolulu Star-Bulletin*, 1925.

"Voyage of the *Roderick Dhu* Marred by Fatal Accident," *San Francisco Call*, January 11, 1896.

"Uncle Sam's Life-Savers at San Francisco," *The Overland Monthly*, 1911.

Flavel – **December 14, 1923**

"A.B. Hammond, West Coast Lumberman," *Journal of Forest History*, October 1984.

"Big Battle on for Right to Salvage the Wreck of Steam Schooner *Flavel*," *Peninsula Daily Herald*, December 15, 1923.

"Big Lumber Schooner Goes on the Rocks," *Peninsula Daily Herald*, December 14, 1923.

"*Flavel* Brings Nitrate," *Humboldt Standard*, October 9, 1918.

"*Flavel* Goes on Rocks," *Humboldt Standard*, December 14, 1923.

"*Flavel* Launched," *Humboldt Standard*, March 3, 1917.

Kuckens, Ben. Interview with the author, October 25, 2012.

"Lifeboat #2, SS *Lahaina*," personal observations of Third Assistant Engineer Michael P. Locke, September 2, 2006.

"Lumber Steamer *Flavel*," *Redwood City Tribune*, December 14, 1923.

"Mayor 'Sunny Jim' Rolph," *Found SF*, September 2012.

"New Steamer *Flavel* Departs," *Humboldt Standard*, March 10, 1917.

"Pacific Coast Steam Schooners," *Power Ships*, Spring 2012.

"Schooner *Flavel* of S.F. Goes on Rocks in Heavy Gale," unidentified clipping, December 14, 1923.

"Schooner Wreck Broken Up and Ship Goes Down," *Peninsula Daily Herald*, December 17, 1923.

"Shipwreck," *What's Doing*, February 1947.

Worthen, James. *Governor James Rolph and the Great Depression in California*. Jefferson, North Carolina: McFarland & Company, 2006.

Frank H. Buck – May 3, 1924

"Blame Shifted in Grounding of Oil Tanker," *San Francisco Chronicle*, May 5, 1924.

"*Coolidge*, Tanker Crash," *San Francisco Chronicle*, March 7, 1937.

"Crash Unavoidable," *San Francisco Chronicle*, March 9, 1937.

"*Frank H. Buck*," *Coast Seamen's Journal*, February 11, 1914.

"*Frank H. Buck*," *Coast Seamen's Journal*, February 18, 1914.

"Oil Tanker Digging Own Grave Off Gate," *San Francisco Chronicle*, March 7, 1937.

"Oil Tanker Wrecked by *President Coolidge* in Collision Beneath Golden Gate Bridge," *Oakland Tribune*, March 7, 1937.

"Old Picture Recalls Impossible Wreck," unidentified clipping, September 1957.

"Pioneer Captain Tells of Fog," *San Francisco Chronicle*, March 12, 1937.

"Shipwreck," *What's Doing*, February 1947.

"Stranded Oil Tanker Pulls Self Off Rocks," *San Francisco Chronicle*, May 18, 1924.

"Stricken Ship Beats Ocean: On Mud Bank," *San Francisco Chronicle*, March 8, 1937.

"Tanker *Frank H. Buck* Stranded on Rocks in Monterey Moved," *San Francisco Chronicle*, May 17, 1924.

"Tanker on the Rocks," *Coast Gazette*, April 16, 1981.

"The Evil Spirits off the California Coast," *Herald Weekend Magazine*, April 14, 1985.

William H. Smith – February 23, 1933

"A Shipbuilding Corporation," *New York Times*, February 13, 1884.

"Beryl Otis Cochran," *Monterey County Herald*, October 26, 2003.

"Career Earned Tulee Iron Man," *Marine Salon*, April 28, 1943.

Cobb, John N. *Pacific Salmon Fisheries*. Washington, D.C.: Government Printing Office, 1921.

"General Thomas W. Hyde Dead," *New York Times*, November 15, 1899.

"High Gale Wrecks Sailing Schooner," *Pacific Grove Tribune*, February 24, 1933.

"Horace Cochran," *Monterey Peninsula Herald*, June 21, 1969.

Little, George Thomas. *Genealogical and Family History of the State of Maine*. New York, New York: Lewis Historical Publishing Company, 1909.

"Maine Shipyards," *Marine Review*, 1899.

Mjelde, Michael Jay. *Glory of the Seas*. Middletown, Connecticut: Wesleyan University Press, 1970.

"New England News," *Boston Evening Transcript*, May 20, 1890.

"Panic Charge Held False at *San Juan* Tragedy Quiz," *San Francisco Examiner*, August 31, 1929.

Ryckman, John W. *Report on the International Maritime Exhibition, Boston 1889-90*. Boston, Massachusetts: Rockwell and Churchill, 1890.

"Sailing Ship Driven Ashore," *Monterey Herald*, February 24, 1933.

"Ship Sank in Minutes," *San Francisco Call Bulletin*, September 3, 1929.

CG-256 – **September 25, 1933**

"Alameda Wreck Inquiry Ended by Inspectors," *San Francisco Call*, October 12, 1905.

Allen, Everett S. *The Black Ships: Rumrunners of Prohibition*. Boston: Little, Brown and Company, 1979.

"All Are Sent Ashore Safely," *San Francisco Call*, October 1, 1905.

Kemp, Michael Kenneth. *Cannery Row: The History of Old Ocean View Avenue*. Pacific Grove, California: The History Company, 1986.

"One of the Heaviest Fogs," *Santa Cruz Sentinel*, January 9, 1925.

"Peter Nelson," *Monterey Peninsula Herald*, April 25, 1964.

"Point Pinos Light Keeper Will Retire," *Monterey Peninsula Herald*, December 22, 1938.

"Rum War: The U.S. Coast Guard and Prohibition," Donald L. Canney, January 1998.

Severn, Bill. *The End of the Roaring Twenties*. New York: Julian Messner, 1969.

"U.S. Cutter Cracks Up on the Rocks," *Monterey Trader*, September 25, 1933.

Willoughby, Malcolm. *Rum War at Sea*. Washington, D.C.: U.S. Government Printing Office, 1964.

J.B. Stetson – **September 3, 1934**

"Captain Appeals Case," *Humboldt Standard*, July 16, 1906.

"Captain Bonifield Exonerated," *Humboldt Standard*, July 24, 1906.

"Earl Hicks a Suicide," *Eugene Register Guard*, September 11, 1913.

"Freight Report," *Pacific Marine Review*, January 1918.

Jackson, J. Hugh and Wheeler, Charles L. *Tide, Time and Lumber*. Palo Alto, California: Stanford University Press, 1949.

"*J.B. Stetson* is Breaking Up off Cypress Point," unidentified clipping, September 3, 1934.

"*J.B. Stetson*'s First Trip," *Humboldt Standard*, June 28, 1909.

"Lumber for War Zone," *Humboldt Standard*, November 30, 1918.

"Lumber Schooner Believed Held Too Tightly to be Salvaged," *San Francisco Examiner*, September 4, 1934.

"Making Good Time with Tow," *Humboldt Standard*, January 16, 1912.

"Pacific Coast Marine," *Coast Seamen's Journal*, September 6, 1916.

"Pounding to Pieces on Monterey Rocks," *San Francisco Examiner*, September 3, 1934.

"San Francisco," *The Timberman*, November 1913.

"Schooner *Stetson* Sold," *San Francisco Examiner*, March 3, 1923.

"Seamen Pay Praise to Bravery," *San Francisco Call*, January 17, 1912.

"S.F. Ship Breaks Up on Rocks off Cypress Point, 20 Saved" *San Francisco Call Bulletin*, September 3, 1934.

"Ship Breaks Up Quickly on Monterey Rocks," unidentified clipping, September 3, 1934.

"Ship on Reef is Abandoned, Crew Rescued," *San Francisco Examiner*, September 3, 1934.

"Shipping," *The Timberman*, November 1913.

"Shipwreck Off Monterey Left to Doom," *San Francisco Chronicle*, September 4, 1934.

"Skipper Battles, Dying, for Helm," *San Francisco Chronicle*, March 27, 1911.

"*Stetson* Arrives with Tow," *Humboldt Standard*, January 17, 1912.

"*Stetson* Wants Big Salvage," *Humboldt Standard*, January 18, 1912.

Wilson, Emily M. *From Boats to Board Feet*. Seattle, Washington: Wilson Brothers Family Foundation, 2007.

"Wrecked Ship Broken in Two," unidentified clipping, September 3, 1934.

OTHER SHIPWRECKS

Bonita – November 12, 1907

"The Central Coast's Narrow-Gauge Lifeline," *Alta Vista Magazine*, May 10, 1992.

"Sails Between Shore Battery and Target while Nearing Port," *San Francisco Call*, November 12, 1907.

"Steamer *Bonita* Held on Rocks but is Saved," *San Francisco Call*, November 13, 1907.

Ida May – August 29, 1930

Department of Commerce. *Annual List of Merchant Vessels and Losses*. Washington, D.C.: Government Printing Office, 1931.

"Commercial Fishing on Mendocino Coast to be Big Industry," *Ferndale Enterprise*, November 13, 1917.

"Eight Sailors Have Miraculous Escape," *San Francisco Chronicle*, February 15, 1930.

"Fishing Schooner Strikes *Princess*," *Victoria Daily Colonist*, October 8, 1908

"Lightkeepers Part of History," *North Island Gazette*, December 7, 1994.

"Pacific Halibut Schooners and Their Builders," *The Sea Chest*, March 1988.

"Pacific Net & Twine," *Pacific Motor Boat*, October 1919.

"Schooner Blew Up," *Montreal Gazette*, April 23, 1908.

"Schooner Run Down," *Dawson Daily News*, October 9, 1908.

Tamalpais – **March 21, 1931**

"Among the Redwoods," *The Timberman*, November 1915.

"List of Steam Schooners Back to 1921," *West Coast Sailor*, November 13, 1953.

"Marine Mishaps," *Weekly Commercial News*, December 4, 1920.

"On Sandbar at Moss Landing," *Santa Cruz Evening News*, March 23, 1931.

"Rescue Ships Aid Disabled Schooner," *Berkeley Daily Gazette*, March 25, 1931.

Italia – **March 2, 1933**

"Point Joe's Reef Takes Two Lives," *Monterey Trader*, March 2, 1933.

Aurora – **January 18, 1935**

"High Gale Wrecks Sailing Schooner," *Pacific Grove Tribune*, February 24, 1933.

Lyman, John. *Pacific Coast-Built Sailers, 1850-1905*. Seattle, Washington: Marine Digest, 1941.

"Rough Times on the Barkentine *Aurora*," *Sea Letter*, August 1972.

"Sailing Ship Driven Ashore," *Monterey Herald*, February 24, 1933.

"Shipwreck," *What's Doing*, February 1947.

New Crivello – **September 18, 1936**

"*New Crivello* Towed To S.F.," *Monterey Peninsula Herald*, September 22, 1936.

"Point Pinos Fog Signal Modernized," *Monterey Peninsula Herald*, July 14, 1939.

"Purse Seiner Total Loss," *Monterey Peninsula Herald*, September 25, 1936.

"Seiner Drifts Ashore On Reefs," *Monterey Peninsula Herald*, September 19, 1936.

YP-128 – June 30, 1942

Cressman, Robert J. *The Official Chronicle of the U.S. Navy in World War II*. Annapolis, Maryland: Naval Institute Press, 2000.

War Diary, Surface Forces, Northern Sector, Western Sea Frontier Patrol Forces, Local Defense Forces, Twelfth Naval District, June 30, 1942.

War Diary, Surface Forces, Northern Sector, Western Sea Frontier Patrol Forces, Local Defense Forces, Twelfth Naval District, July 1, 1942.

War Diary, Surface Forces, Northern Sector, Western Sea Frontier Patrol Forces, Local Defense Forces, Twelfth Naval District, July 2, 1942.

Amphibious Craft – June 7, 1944

Skaarup, Harold A. *Florida Warbird Survivors*. Writers Club Press: Lincoln, Nebraska, 2001.

War Diary, U.S. Pacific Fleet, Blimp Squadron 32, U.S. Naval Air Station, Moffett Field, California, June 12, 1944.

War Diary, U.S. Pacific Fleet, Blimp Squadron 32, U.S. Naval Air Station, Moffett Field, California, July 1, 1944.

Yiede, Harry. *The Infantry's Armor*. Mechanicsburg, Pennsylvania: Stackpole Books, 2010.

INDEX